The Complete

Friday Evening

Synagogue Companion

THE
JEWISH
LEARNING GROUP

THE COMPLETE FRIDAY EVENING SYNAGOGUE COMPANION

Previously published under the title
THE COMPLETE KABBALAT SHABBAT SYNAGOGUE COMPANION

Copyright © 1996-2019

THE
JEWISH
LEARNING GROUP

Tel. 1-(888)-56-LEARN
www.JewishLearningGroup.com
Email: Info@JewishLearningGroup.com

ISBN-10: 1-891293-14-1
ISBN-13: 978-1-891293-14-6

Acknowledgements

A special thanks to Rabbi-Dr. Nissan Mindel, editor-in-chief of Kehot Publication Society, for permitting the use of portions from his popular book, *My Prayer;* and to Jay Litvin for his inspiring essay.

To Rabbi Sholom Ber Chaikin, for giving selflessly of his valuable time to read, amend, and refine the material presented.

To Rabbi Shmuel Rabin for proofreading.

To the countless Rabbis and lay-leaders who have offered their creative ideas, advice, and never-ending encouragement.

To everyone else who helped make this title such a popular staple in synagogues across the globe.

We have devised the following transliteration system to help readers accurately pronounce the Hebrew words of blessings and prayers presented in this book.

Hebrew:	Transliteration:	Example:
ח or כ	ch	Challah
ָ	ö	Of
־	a	Hurrah
�‥	ay	Today
ֶ	e	Leg
ְ	'	Avid
ֹ or וֹ	o	Tone
�/	i	Key
ֻ or וּ	u	Lunar
ַי	ai	Aisle
ָי	öy	Toy

Table of Contents

A Quick Shabbat Primer

What is Shabbat?

Shabbat is not just the seventh day of the week or the day on which God rested from creating the world. It is much more than that. Shabbat was made by God as a day unto itself. It has its own identity. It is not just a day meant to be absent of work; unencumbered by our daily distractions, the day of Shabbat is to be used to connect with our spiritual source. Shabbat is also a day on which we stand proudly as Jews, proud to be God's light unto the nations, proud to be the bearers of God's way of life.

We also utilize the Shabbat day to stop, stand back, and appreciate God's creation, and spend time calibrating our "spiritual compass" for the coming week. For the 25 hours of Shabbat we cease interacting with the material world. We stop working and creating, all in order to pause and acknowledge the real Creator, lest we become too self-absorbed in our daily grind to remember that all our fortune comes from God, and realize that our work is only a vessel to receive His bountiful blessings.

On Shabbat we remember our main goal and purpose in this world: we're here not only to achieve fame, accumulate riches, or advance technology, but also to refine the material world we live in.

This is accomplished by following and living by the ways of the Torah, given to us by God, over 3,300 years ago at Mount Sinai.

What better way to spend this holy day than with family and friends, immersing ourselves in prayer and Torah study, and maximizing this golden opportunity which comes to us only once a week.

Keeping an Authentic Shabbat

There are many laws and guidelines found in the Torah and Codes of Jewish Law regarding the proper observance of Shabbat. Since Shabbat is God's gift to the Jewish people, we observe it as God wants us to, not merely on our own terms. This means adhering to the proper way Shabbat was practiced by Jews for thousands of years. Many helpful books have been written that explain these laws, and are available in Jewish bookstores. They can help you learn more about the Shabbat and assist you as you embark on this wonderful spiritual journey.

The Message of Shabbat

To obtain a deeper insight into the special nature of Shabbat, what it means to us, and what is its universal message, we will dwell briefly on the main aspects of the Shabbat, particularly those that are reflected in Shabbat prayers.

The Torah tells us that God created the world in six days, and that by the end of the sixth day the heaven and earth and all their hosts were completed. Then God rested from all creative activity, *"and God blessed the seventh day and made it holy."* Thus, right from the beginning of Creation God has set the Shabbat day apart from the other days of the week as a holy day. But for whom was the Shabbat meant? Who was to accept it, appreciate it, and keep it holy? The answer is found in the

following meaningful Midrash:

"Rabbi Shimon bar Yochai taught: When God created the holy Shabbat, it said to the Holy One, blessed be He: "Every day You created has a mate. Am I to be the only odd one, without a mate?" Replied God, "The Jewish people will be your mate." And so, while the Jewish people stood at the foot of Mount Sinai to receive the Torah and become a nation, God declared (in the Ten Commandments): "Remember the Shabbat day, to keep it holy!" As if to say, "Remember My promise to the Shabbat that the Jewish nation shall be its mate."

Jewish mystical teachings refer to the Jewish people and the Shabbat in terms of bridegroom and bride, and this is why in the Shabbat prayers, the Shabbat is welcomed with the words, *Bo-i chalöh, Bo-i chalöh* — "Welcome, bride; welcome, bride!" The repetition, *Bo-i chalöh*, alludes to the two great qualities of the "bride," being both "blessed" and "holy," as it is written, "And God blessed the seventh day and made it holy." Indeed, according to Rabbi Yitzchak Arama in his *Akedat Yitzchak*, the word *L'kadsho* — "to keep it holy" — may be rendered "to betroth it," in the sense of *kiddushin,* marriage.

In this way, our sages tell us that the Shabbat is uniquely Jewish, that is to say, that the Jewish people and the Shabbat are inseparable; they were destined for each other from the moment of their "birth." Without the Shabbat the Jewish people is simply unthinkable, just as without the Torah, the Jewish people is unthinkable. This is one of the reasons why the Shabbat is equated with all the mitzvot.

Shabbat in the Torah

The origin of the Shabbat, referred to as the Shabbat of Creation, is given in the section of *Vayechulu* in the Bible (see Genesis 2,1), which is also recited during Shabbat services. Shabbat is not mentioned again explicitly in the Torah until after the story of the Exodus, in connection with the manna. This heavenly bread did not come down on the Shabbat, but instead, the children of Israel received a double portion on Friday for Shabbat as well. Then Moses told the children of Israel, *"See, God has given you this Shabbat."*

The Shabbat was nothing new for the children of Israel, for, as our sages tell us, they had known about it traditionally from the time of Abraham and, indeed, observed it even in Egypt. On this occasion, however, they received the first laws about Shabbat, and several weeks later, they received formal instructions on Shabbat in the Ten Commandments at Mount Sinai.

After the Torah was given to our people, the commandment to observe the Shabbat is repeated in the Torah many times with great emphasis. One of the better known passages about the Shabbat is included in the Shabbat morning prayers: *"And the children of Israel shall keep the Shabbat…as an everlasting covenant. It is a sign between Me and the children of Israel forever: That in six days God made heaven and earth, and on the seventh day He ceased from work and rested."*

Here the Torah tells us of the basic significance of the Shabbat as the living sign of God's creation. By keeping the Shabbat, we, the Jewish people, proclaim for the world that God is the Creator of heaven and

earth, and we reaffirm the everlasting covenant between God and the Jewish people.

God has crowned His creation with the Shabbat, and has given this crown to us. Our sages of the Talmud expressed it this way, *"A precious gift —says God— have I in My treasure stores; its name is Shabbat, and I have given it to you."*

Wearing this crown is, of course, a great privilege. But it also places upon us great responsibilities. These are summed up by Rambam (Maimonides) as follows:

"The Shabbat is the everlasting sign between God and the people of Israel...He who observes the Shabbat properly, honoring it and delighting in it to the best of his ability, is given a reward in this world, over and above the reward that is reserved for him in the World to Come."

Shabbat and Jewish Identity

More than anything else, it has been the Shabbat that has distinguished the Jewish people from all other nations of the world, for Shabbat observance is not just a matter of a single precept or custom, but something that is fundamental to the Jewish religion and Jewish way of life.

During Shabbat, a Jew not only desists from work, closes down his store, factory, or workshop and halts all work at home, but is completely transformed into a person of holiness, devoting the time to prayer and study. Even externally this transformation is in evidence, in one's dress, eating, walking, and talking.

For thousands of years the nations of the world could not understand this Jewish Shabbat. They, who had not known a rest day in the week altogether, thought it deplorable for an entire nation to take off work for a whole day in the week. When Haman complained to King Ahasuerus about the "one people, scattered and dispersed among the nations, whose laws are different from those of any other nation," it was Shabbat and the festivals that he held up to ridicule. Ancient Roman historians called the Jewish people "lazy" and "uncivilized" for their adherence to the Shabbat.

When the nations of the world finally recognized the Torah as a holy book, and called it "The Book" (Bible), they adopted some of its principles. They also introduced a "Sabbath" or "day of rest" into their religions. But it is significant that they made it on Sunday (in Christianity), or on Friday (in Islam). The Shabbat remained Jewish for Jews alone. Although imitation may be the highest form of flattery, nothing in the imitations can approach the original, Divinely ordained Shabbat, as anyone familiar with the laws of Shabbat and their significance knows.

A Remembrance of the Exodus from Egypt

In the Shabbat sanctification ceremony that we conduct upon arriving home from Friday evening services, known as the Kiddush, we thank God for giving us the Shabbat "as a memorial to the work of Creation" and also "as a remembrance of the Exodus from Egypt." These two basic perceptions of Shabbat are derived from the Ten Commandments, the fourth of which deals with Shabbat.

$\mathcal{A}$ Quick Shabbat Primer

In the first Decalogue (Exodus 20) it is stated: *"Remember the Shabbat day...for in six days God made heaven and earth, the sea and all that is in them, and ceased work on the seventh day; wherefore God blessed the Shabbat day and sanctified it."* The text in the second Decalogue (Deuteronomy 5) reads: *"Observe the Shabbat day to keep it holy...And you shall remember that you were a slave in the land of Egypt, and God your God brought you out of there by a mighty hand and by an outstretched arm; therefore, God your God commanded you to keep the Shabbat day."*

Commenting on the different aspects of Shabbat as reflected in the Ten Commandments in Exodus and Deuteronomy respectively, the Ramban (Nachmanides) explains that, far from being contra- dictory, they are supportive and complementary. For as the day of rest attesting to the Creation, Shabbat also brings to mind the time when the Jewish people, being enslaved in Egypt, were not free to rest on that day. They had to work on all seven days of the week. Hence, the Torah emphasizes, *"in order that your manservant and your maidservant may rest as well as you."*

In a deeper sense, the Ramban continues, the Exodus from Egypt confirmed and deepened our belief without doubt in God as Creator of the universe. Until the Exodus from Egypt, the belief in One God came down to the Jewish people from Abraham, Isaac and Jacob, the founders of our Jewish nation, along with the unique covenant that had been established between God and the Patriarchs and their descendants. During the centuries of enslavement, however, belief and tradition were put to severe test.

13

Many, if not most, of the enslaved Jews must have had some doubts whether there really was a Supreme Being, Creator and Master of the world, or if such a Being had not abandoned the world to its devices, or to the mighty Pharaohs. The Exodus from Egypt, with all its wonders and miracles, demonstrated without any doubt that God was truly the Creator and Master of the world, since He was able at will to suspend and change the laws of nature.

Moreover, the Exodus from Egypt demonstrated, too, that Divine *Hashgachah* ("watchfulness," personal divine providence) extends to every particular and detail of the created order, to humans as well as to the lower orders of animal and plant life, even to the inanimate.

A third essential element of the Exodus experience was the revelation of prophecy. It established the fact that the Creator not only bestowed upon Moses the gift of prophecy, but made him the greatest of all prophets (forty-eight men and seven women, according to our sages). It was at the miraculous crossing of *Yam Suf* (Red Sea; Sea of Reeds) that the liberated Israelites attained complete trust in God and in Moses His servant — meaning, in the prophecy of Moses His servant.

This belief in the truth of Moses' prophecy is no less a cornerstone of our Jewish faith than the belief in the two fundamental principles mentioned above: namely, the existence of a Supreme Being as Creator of the world, and Divine Providence extending to the smallest detail of the created order. For, although the entire nation witnessed the Divine Revelation at Mount Sinai and heard the Decalogue, the entire Torah with all its 613 mitzvot was transmitted through Moses.

In light of the above, the Ramban points out, we can appreciate the Talmudic declaration that "Shabbat equi-balances all the mitzvot," since by keeping Shabbat we attest to the truth of all the fundamental principles of our faith: Creation *ex nihilo*, Divine Providence and Divine Prophecy.

Thus, Ramban concludes, Shabbat is a remembrance of the Exodus from Egypt, while the Exodus from Egypt, in turn, is a memorial to Shabbat of Creation.

Putting Your Best Into Shabbat

Referring to the above-mentioned verse, *"And the children of Israel shall "keep"* (v'sham'ru) *the Shabbat, to "make"* (la-asos) *the Shabbat,"* etc., our sages declare that to "keep" refers to all the laws pertaining to the cessation of work and all that we may not do on Shabbat; and to "make" refers to all things that we have to put into the Shabbat, to honor it, delight in it and fill it with holiness through prayer and study.

Jews make the Shabbat and Shabbat makes the Jewish people. That is what is meant by referring to the Shabbat and the Jewish people as real mates, as mentioned earlier. Indeed, more than the Jewish people kept the Shabbat, the Shabbat has kept the Jewish people, for more than anything else, the Shabbat unites all Jews, in all parts of the world.

The Shabbat is also a reminder to all mankind that it must persistently move toward the "day that is all Shabbat" — a world where all the nations of the world will recognize the sovereignty of the Creator and His rule on earth, a world in which there is no strife, nor violence,

15

nor injustice, for the spirit of Shabbat (peace) will permeate the whole world.

Enjoying a Richly Satisfying Shabbat

A richly satisfying Shabbat never just happens, it is the result of an effort made all week long. The Talmud tells of a sage who purchased all week in honor of Shabbat. Whenever he saw a special food in the market he would buy it and say, "This is for the Shabbat." When he found something better quality, he would replace the earlier item and say, "This is for the Shabbat." Thus, his whole week was permeated with Shabbat!

Now, Shabbat preparations do not only surround food. There are many other preparations that must be done before the onset of the Shabbat at sundown on Friday. For a fuller understanding of these, refer to the Laws of Shabbat section of the "Code of Jewish Law." For introductory purposes, a few of the major points are presented below.

CLOTHING

It is customary to have special clothes for Shabbat. Traditionally this means a white shirt and long dark pants or suit for men and boys, and a modest dress for woman and girls. In fact, many people set aside their nicest suit or dress and wear it only on the Shabbat. In that way, it's obvious to all that Shabbat is a special day.

FOOD

There are three meals eaten on Shabbat. 1) Friday night after the services, 2) Shabbat morning after the services, and 3) late Shabbat

afternoon. The table is traditionally decked with a white tablecloth. Some place the Shabbat candles on the dining table (at candle lighting) to enjoy the radiant light of Shabbat during the meal. The finest cutlery, dishes and silverware are also brought out and used.

Among the many traditional foods prepared for the Shabbat, you will find special braided bread called challa, along with dishes of fish, meat, and tasty wines. This is no random selection. This order of foods was handed down to us by our sages, and this precept was extracted from the commandment in the Torah, *"to honor the Shabbat with food and drink."*

Appropriate food for the Shabbat is so important that we are taught that one who cannot afford to purchase any of the above food items, should borrow the money to purchase them!

WORK

As you know by now, Shabbat is a day of rest, and as discussed earlier, this rest is not only a "quiet time," to rejuvenate our energies. While this may also be the case, the rest on Shabbat means the cessation of any creative function we normally do during the week. This is to enable us to recognize and appreciate the One who really does the creating, our God in Heaven.

Practically (and very generally) this means that Jewish people are prohibited from performing any actions associated with the Torah's list of 39 forbidden activities on Shabbat.

This includes cooking or lighting fires, driving a car or motorcycle, shopping, handling money, turning lights on or off (lighting a fire), using phones, fax machines, watching TV, going to the movies, playing

golf or tennis, sewing, rowing, swimming, skating, boating, flying, barbecuing, etc.

What's left to do?

A young person came to a Jewish sage and asked, "Why are there so many restrictions on the Shabbat? I feel so imprisoned! I can't watch TV, I can't use the phone, I can't turn on lights, I can't go to the mall."

"Did you hear me say the word prohibited?" the Rabbi asked.

"What do you mean, Rabbi? You taught us that on Shabbat you can't do this and can't do that, and that is how one guards the sanctity of the Shabbat."

The sage replied, "My son, what I said was that on Shabbat you are permitted *not* to watch TV, *not* to answer the phones, *not* to check for email, *not* to cook. You are truly free to rest. This is most liberating, not imprisoning!"

Indeed, when was the last time that you felt free to shut out the world and be yourself with your friends, family, and, yes, your Creator? That's what Shabbat is all about! After observing Shabbat and "tuning-out" the world and "tuning-in" to our family and spirituality, you'll feel the happiness, satisfaction, and fulfillment that Shabbat offers everyone who observes it properly.

Our sages relate that Shabbat "takes" from the Friday before and extends into the Saturday night after. We can't just go directly into Shabbat; we have to prepare ourselves beforehand.

At the same time, we don't end Shabbat on the dot of sunset on Saturday, but bring some of the Shabbat atmosphere with us into the Saturday evening.

SELF

We spend part of Shabbat day in prayer, a part learning Torah, and a part enjoying the people who are important to us. Shabbat is also an opportune time to do "spiritual accounting." We focus on how we can better ourselves during the week to come.

FAMILY

Shabbat is often called "the glue that keeps the family together." On this day, families spend time eating and sharing thoughts with one another. On Shabbat, it is also customary for parents to learn topics of Jewish values with their children.

A Quick Prayer Primer

Connecting With the Prayer Services

It may be your first time in a synagogue, or the hundredth, but the feeling may be the same. You say to yourself, 'I like it here, it feels good and I know I am doing the right thing, but I don't feel as if I am *really* participating, I don't feel that I really *connect*.'

You may find comfort in knowing that an average middle-age observant Jew has prayed over 30,000 prayer services (three times a day, on average). It's no wonder it appears to be so easy for some. Imagine how the Speaker of the House feels on his first day on his job in the Congress and how comfortable he becomes at the end of his term. He memorized the protocol, he feels at home.

So don't beat yourself up so much if on your tenth, or even hundredth time to the synagogue you feel like a young child in Einstein's lab. This is normal, and most importantly, this book will help you learn exactly what you can do about it.

Let's Talk Some Shop

From our school years we can remember our parents and teachers telling us that proper preparation saves lots of perspiration. And as much as we hated to hear it, they were right. So, to make our parents proud,

we'll start at the beginning and prepare ourselves for our next visit to the synagogue. Let's start by defining "prayer." Prayer is a big word, it carries a lot of baggage. One person may conjure up an image of a servant and his master; another may think of prayer as something you do only when in trouble; a student might think back to the day of his college finals. But, what do we, as Jews, believe and know about prayer?

Why Do Jews Pray?

Prayer is a commandment of God. We are told to pray to Him for our needs, and in our prayers we often address God as our Merciful Father, or as our Father in Heaven, for God regards us, and we regard ourselves, as His children. You may ask, Why do we have to pray to God for our needs? Doesn't God know our needs even better than we do ourselves? Is not God, by His very nature, good and kind, and always willing to do us good? After all, children do not "pray" to their parents to feed them, and clothe them, and protect them; why should we pray to our Heavenly Father for such things?

The answer to these questions is not hard to find after a little reflection. It has been amply explained by our wise Sages, including the great teacher and guide, Maimonides. He lived some 800 years ago, and was one of the greatest codifiers of Jewish law. He wrote the following concerning prayer:

"We are told to offer up prayers to God, in order to establish firmly the true principle that God takes notice of our ways, that He can make them successful if we serve Him, or disastrous if we disobey Him; that success and failure are not the result of chance or accident."

A Quick Prayer Primer

As is the case with all other commandments that God has given to the Jewish people, the commandment to pray is not only for His sake but for ours.

And you are right, God does not "need" our prayers; He can do without our prayers, but *we* cannot do without our prayers. It is good for *us* to acknowledge *our* dependence on God for our very life, our health, our daily bread, and our general welfare. We do so every day, and many times a day. We need to remind ourselves that our life and happiness are a gift from our Creator, and in turn we try to be worthy of God's kindnesses and favors to us.

God does not owe us anything; yet He gives us everything. We should try to do the same for our fellow men and grant favors freely. We should express our gratitude to God not merely in words, but in deeds: By obeying His commands and living our daily life the way God wants us to — especially because it is all for our own good.

Knowing that God is good and that nothing is impossible for Him to do, we can go about our life with a deep sense of confidence and security. Even in times of distress we will not despair, knowing that in some way (best known to God) whatever happens to us is for our own good. It is a blessing in disguise.

Nevertheless, we pray to God to help us out of our distress, and grant us the good that is not hidden or disguised. That He give us the good that is obvious even to humans who have limited understanding.

We gain strength, courage and hope by trusting in God, and our daily prayers strengthen this trust in God. "In God We Trust" has been our Jewish motto since we first became a people.

23

Going a Bit Deeper

The Hebrew word תפלה (*tefillah*) is generally translated as "prayer," but this is not an accurate translation. To pray means to beg, beseech, implore and the like, and we have a number of Hebrew words that more accurately convey this meaning. Our daily prayers are not merely requests to God to give us our daily needs and nothing more. Of course, such requests are also included in our prayers, but mostly our prayers are much more than that, as we shall see.

Reaching Upwards

Our Sages declare that the ladder which our forefather Jacob saw in his dream, with angels of God "going up and coming down," was also the symbol of prayer. By showing the ladder to Jacob in his dream, a ladder which "stood on the earth and reached into the heaven," our Sages explain, God showed Jacob that prayer is like a ladder which connects the earth with the heaven — man with God.

The meaningful words of prayer, the good resolutions which it brings forth, are transformed into angels that go to God, Who then sends them down with blessings in return. That is why Jacob saw in his dream that angels were "going up and coming down," although one would have expected angels to first come down and *then* go up.

Thus, what we said about prayer in answer to the question: "Why do we pray?" is but the first step on the "ladder" of prayer. Prayer also has to do with things that are on a higher level than daily material needs — namely spiritual things.

24

A Time of Self-Judgment

The Hebrew word תפלה (*tefillah*) comes from the verb פלל (*pallel*), "to judge." The reflexive verb להתפלל (*lehitpallel*) "to pray" also means, "to judge oneself." Thus, the time of prayer is a time of self-judgment and self-evaluation.

When a person addresses himself to God and prays for His blessings, he must inevitably search his heart and examine whether he measures up to the standards of daily conduct which God has prescribed for man to follow. If he is honest with himself, he will be filled with humility, realizing that he hardly merits the blessings and favors for which he is asking. This is why we stress in our prayers God's infinite goodness and mercies. We pray to God to grant us our heart's desires, not because we merit them, but even though we may not deserve them.

This is also why our prayers, on weekdays, contain a confession of sins which we may have committed, knowingly or unknowingly. We pray for God's forgiveness, and resolve to better ourselves.

So we see how prayer can also help us lead a better life in every respect, by living more fully the way of the Torah and mitzvot, which God commanded us.

The Ultimate Service

On an even higher level, prayer becomes עבודה (*avodah*), "service." The Torah commands us "to serve God with our hearts," and our Sages say: "What kind of service is 'service of the heart?' — it is prayer." In this sense, prayer is meant to purify our hearts and our nature.

The plain Hebrew meaning of *avodah* is "work." We work with a raw material and convert it into a refined and finished product. In the process, we remove the impurities, or roughness, of the raw material, whether it is a piece of wood or a rough diamond, and make it into a thing of usefulness or beauty.

The tanner, for example, takes raw hide and converts it into fine leather. The parchment on which a Torah Scroll, a *Mezuzah*, or *Tefillin* is written, is made of the hide of a kosher animal. Raw wool full of grease and other impurities, through stages of "work," is made into a fine wool from which we can make not only fine clothes, but also a *Tallit* (prayer shawl), or *Tzitzit* (fringed garment).

Diamond in the Rough

The Jewish people have been likened in the Torah to soil and earth, and have been called God's "land of desire." The saintly Ba'al Shem Tov, the founder of Chassidism, explained it this way: The earth is full of treasures, but they are often buried deep inside. It is necessary to dig for them; and when you discover them, you still have to clear away the impurities, refine them or polish them, as in the case of gold or diamonds.

Similarly, every Jew is full of wonderful treasures of character — modesty, kindness and other natural traits — but sometimes they are buried deep and covered up by "soil" and "dust," which have to be cleared away.

Character Refinery

We speak of a person of good character as a "refined" person, or of "refined" character. It is often difficult, to overcome such bad traits as pride, anger, jealousy, which may be quite "natural" but are still unbecoming for a human being, especially for a Jew.

Tefillah, in the sense of *avodah*, is the "refinery" where the impurities of character are done away with. These bad character traits stem from the "animal" soul in man, and are "natural" to it. But we are endowed with a "Divine" soul, which is a spark of Godliness itself, and the treasure of all the wonderful qualities which make a man superior to an animal.

During proper prayer, our Divine soul speaks to God, and even the animal soul is filled with holiness. We realize that we stand before the Holy One, blessed be He, and the whole material world with all its pains and pleasures seems to melt away. We become aware of things that really matter and are truly important; even as we pray for life, health and sustenance, we think of these things in their deeper sense: a life that is worthy to be called "living"; health that is not only physical, but above all spiritual; sustenance — the things that truly sustain us in this world and in the world to come — the Torah and mitzvot.

We feel cleansed and purified by such service, and when we return to our daily routine, the feeling of purity and holiness lingers and raises our daily conduct to a level fitting for a member of the people called a "kingdom of priests and a holy nation."

Complete Attachment to God

The highest level on the "ladder" of prayer is reached when we are so inspired as to want nothing but the feeling of attachment with God. On this level *tefillah* is related to the verb (used in Mishnaic Hebrew) תופל (*tofel*), to "attach," "join," or "bind together," as two pieces of a broken vessel are pieced together to make it whole again.

Our soul is truly a part of God, and therefore longs to be reunited with, and reabsorbed in, Godliness. Just as a small flame when it is put close to a larger flame, is absorbed into the larger flame. We may not always be aware of this longing, but it is there nonetheless.

Our soul has, in fact, been called the "candle of God." The flame of a candle is restless, striving upwards, to break away, as it were, from the wick and body of the candle; for such is the nature of fire — to strive upwards. Our soul, too, strives upwards, like that flame. This is also one of the reasons why a Jew naturally sways while praying. For prayer is the means whereby we attach ourselves to God, with a soulful attachment of "spirit to spirit," and in doing so our soul flutters and soars upward, to be united with God.

Mitzvah Means Connection

Let us examine this idea more closely. Every mitzvah which God has commanded us to do, and which we perform as a sacred commandment, attaches us to God. The word mitzvah is related to the Aramaic word צוותא (*tzavta*), "togetherness," or "company." In English, too, we have the verb "to enjoin," which means "to command," for the commandment

is the bond that joins together the person commanded with the person commanding, no matter how far apart they may be in distance, rank or position.

When a king commands a humble servant to do something, this establishes a bond between the two. The humble servant feels greatly honored that the king has taken notice of him and has given him something to do, and that he, an insignificant person, can do something to please the great king. It makes him eager to be worthy of the king's attention and favor.

If this is so in the case of every mitzvah, it is even more so in the case of prayer. For nothing brings us closer to God than prayer, when it is truly the outpouring of the soul and, therefore, makes for an "attachment of spirit to spirit," as mentioned earlier. If any mitzvah brings us closer to God, prayer (on the level we are speaking) is like being embraced by God. There is no greater pleasure or fulfillment than the wonderful spiritual uplift and blissfulness resulting from prayer.

The Order of Prayers

Prayer, we said, is like a "ladder" of many rungs. To get to the top of it, we must start at the bottom and steadily rise upwards. To enable us to do so, our prayers have been composed prophetically by our saintly Prophets and Sages of old, and have been ordered also like a "ladder," steadily leading us to greater and greater inspiration. We must, therefore, become familiar with our prayers: first of all their plain meaning, then their deeper meaning, and finally the whole "order" of the service.

The Three Daily Prayers

Jewish Law requires us to pray three times daily: Morning, afternoon and evening. These prayers are called *Shacharit* (morning prayer), *Minchah* (afternoon prayer), and *Arvit*, or *Maariv* (evening prayer), respectivly.

Our Sages tell us that our Patriarchs, Abraham, Isaac and Jacob originally introduced the custom of praying three times a day. Abraham introduced prayer in the morning; Isaac instituted afternoon prayer, and Jacob added one at night.

In the *Zohar* (or *kabbalah*; the mystical part of the Torah) it is explained further that each of the three Patriarchs represented a particular quality which they introduced into the service of God. Abraham served God with love; Isaac with awe; and Jacob with mercy. Not that each lacked the qualities of the others, but each had a particular quality that was more prominent.

Thus Abraham distinguished himself especially in the quality of kindness (חסד) and love (אהבה), while Isaac excelled especially in the quality of strict justice (דין) and reverence (יראה). Jacob inherited both these qualities, bringing out a new quality which combined the first two into the well-balanced and lasting quality of truth (אמת) and mercy (רחמים).

We, the children of Abraham, Isaac and Jacob, have inherited all three great qualities of our Patriarchs, enabling us to serve God and pray to Him with love and fear (awe) and mercy. The quality of mercy comes in when we realize that our soul is a part of Godliness, and we feel pity

for it because it is so often distracted from God by the material aspects of daily life.

Prayer In the Torah

When the Torah was given to us at Mount Sinai, our way of life was set out for us by God. Torah means "teaching," "instruction," "guidance"; for the Torah teaches us our way of living, including every detail of our daily life. The Torah contains 613 commandments. Among them is the command to "serve God with all our heart and all our soul." By praying to Him we fulfill not only the commandment of prayer, but also other commandments, such as to love God and to fear Him.

During the first one thousand years or so from the time of Moshe *Rabbeinu* (Moses), there was no set order of prayer. Each individual was duty-bound to pray to God every day, but the form of prayer was left to the individual.

There was, however, a set order of service in the *Beit Hamikdash* (the Holy Temple that stood in Jerusalem) in connection with the daily sacrifices, morning and afternoon, with the latter sacrifice extending into the night. On special days, such as Shabbat, *Rosh Chodesh* (start of a new month), and Festivals, there were also "additional" (*musaf*) sacrifices.

Accordingly, it was not unusual for some Jews to pray three times a day — morning, afternoon, and evening — in their own way. King David, for example, declared that he prayed three times daily, and Daniel (in Babylon) prayed three times daily facing the direction of Jerusalem.

31

There is evidence that, even during the time of the first *Beit Hamikdash*, there were public places of prayer, called *Beit Ha-am*, which the Chaldeans (Babylonians) destroyed, along with the *Beit Hamikdash* and the rest of Jerusalem.

Setting the Order of Prayers

After the *Beit Hamikdash* was destroyed and the Jews were led into captivity in Babylon, Jews continued to gather and pray in congregation. The places of prayer became like "small sanctuaries." But during the years of exile, the children that were born and raised in Babylon lacked adequate knowledge of the Holy Tongue, Hebrew, and spoke a mixed language.

Therefore, when the Jews returned to their homeland after the seventy years of exile were over, Ezra the Scribe together with the Men of the Great Assembly (consisting of Prophets and Sages, 120 members in all) set the text of the daily prayer, *Shemoneh Esrei* — the "Eighteen Benedictions," and made it a permanent institution and duty in Jewish life to recite this prayer three times daily.

Ever since then it became part of Jewish Law (*halacha*) for each and every Jew to pray this ordained and fixed order of prayer three times daily, corresponding to the daily sacrifices in the *Beit Hamikdash*, with additional (*Musaf*) prayers on Shabbat, *Rosh Chodesh* and Festivals, and a special "closing" prayer (*Neilah*) on Yom Kippur. Thus, the main parts of the daily prayers were formulated by our Sages, which still are the main parts of our morning and evening prayers.

The *Shema* was included in the morning and evening prayers, and the daily Psalm which used to be sung by the Levites in the *Beit Hamikdash*, became part of the morning prayer. Other Psalms of David were included in the morning prayer, and special benedictions before and after the *Shema* were added. By the time the Mishna was recorded by Rabbi Judah the Prince about the year 3,910 (some 500 years after Ezra; 150 C.E.), and especially by the time the Talmud was completed (some 300 years later, or about 1500 years ago), the basic order of our prayers, as we know them now, had been formulated.

Inside the Prayers

The morning service consists of the following sections:

1) The blessings upon rising from bed.

2) The chapters of praise.

3) The blessings for the *Shema*.

4) The *Shema*.

5) The *Amidah*.

6) The concluding prayers.

1) Upon waking in the morning we express our gratitude to God for the rest we had, for giving us back all our senses and restoring strength to our weary limbs. We thank God also for the great privilege of being a Jew and serving God, for having given us His holy Torah, and so on.

2) Then we recite Psalms of praise to God, describing His majesty and might, as the Creator of Heaven and Earth and all creatures, His loving-kindness and goodness in taking care of all creatures.

3-4) Having thus been inspired by God's goodness and love, we declare the Unity of God, and we take upon ourselves to love God and observe all His commands.

5) After all the above, we come to the main part of the prayer — the *Amidah*, in which we put our requests before God.

6) We then conclude the service with appropriate Psalms and prayers.

This is again one of the reasons why prayer has been likened to a ladder ("Jacob's Ladder") connecting earth and heaven. For the sections of our prayer indeed are like the rungs of a ladder, one leading to the other.

My Time With God

So, as we see from the above, prayer time in the synagogue is too valuable to blow on shmooze, news, and maybe even a little snooze. It is a sacred time of real communion with God, a time of self-analysis and self-growth.

Think of it as being invited to participate in an intricate experiment in a laboratory, or given an opportunity to change things in your own life, and instead one sits lounging with a newspaper or making small talk, all while this great stuff is happening all around us.

So, we are indeed ready to give our attention to the matter at hand in the synagogue, and leave the socializing for later, or the Kiddush that usually follows the services on Shabbat.

You may still ask, "What do we do with all this "new" free time? "How do I turn on this mystic connection with God?"

The "Siddur" Prayer Book

For many years during the period of the Holy Temple (some 2,000 years ago), the Jewish people prayed by heart. As times changed, and younger generations were not learning the prayers, it was time to set them in fixed order in a book. This book was called a *Siddur*. The Siddur became our traditional prayer book, containing the three daily prayers; the prayers for Shabbat, *Rosh Chodesh* and the Festivals.

"Siddur" means "order," since in the Siddur we find our prayers in their proper and fixed order. Sometimes, for the sake of convenience, the Shabbat and *Rosh Chodesh* prayers may be printed in a separate volume. The prayers for Rosh Hashanah and Yom Kippur are usually printed in separate volumes, called *Machzor* ("cycle"). Sometimes the prayers for the Three Festivals — Passover, Shavuot and Sukkot — are also printed in separate volumes.

The oldest Siddur that we know of is the Siddur of Rav *Amram Gaon*, Head of the Yeshiva of Sura, in Babylon, about 1,100 years ago. He had prepared it at the request of the Jews of Barcelona, Spain. It contains the arrangements of the prayers for the entire year, including also some laws concerning prayer and customs. It was copied and used the Jews of

France and Germany, and was in fact the standard prayer book for all Jewish communities.

Seder Rav Amram Gaon remained in handwritten form for about 1,000 years, until it was printed for the first time in Warsaw in 1865. Rav *Saadia Gaon*, who was head of the Sura Yeshiva less than 100 years after Rav Amram Gaon, arranged a Siddur for the Jews in Arab countries, with explanations and instructions in Arabic. The *Rambam*, Maimonides, in his famous Code of Jewish Law, also prepared the order of the prayers for the whole year (including the Haggadah of Passover), and included it in his work, following the section dealing with the laws of prayer.

The structure of the prayers remains basically the same. The morning prayers begin with the morning blessings, continue with *Pesukei D'zimra* (Psalms and sections from the Prophets, introduced and concluded by benedictions), followed by the *Shema* (which is also introduced and concluded by a benediction), and continues with the main prayer, *Shemoneh Esrei*, which means "eighteen," because originally this prayer had eighteen blessings (weekday version), and is also known as the *Amidah* ("standing"), because it must be recited in a standing position.

The Words to Express What's on My Heart

Suppose you were at an event and were asked to stand up and make a speech. Wouldn't it be easier if you had some outline to help you? The Siddur is the book with all the necesary words to kindle within us the feelings we feel. The early rabbis did us the greatest favor by putting it all in order. This is the value of the prayers — their outline, order and sequence, down to the words and letters chosen. They help us

36

experience the befitting emotion. We may not all be poets, but it is indeed difficult to read through the prayers and *not* feel moved at some point or another to feelings of gratitude, awe, solemnity, etc. On one day it will be one prayer that does it. Another time a different one. The experience is always in the words, just waiting for you to activate them.

Feel God, thank God, appreciate what you've got, and ask God to give you strength to pull through for Him, for yourself, and for the entire Jewish people.

Habit or Hobby?

It is easy after a while to read familiar prayers too quickly, or without real concentration. It can become nothing more than a habit. Yet familiarity need not necessarily make it so. For as we know, people eat three times a day and usually enjoy every meal.

So when we pray and give our prayer a little thought, we can find great inspiration and uplift in them. At least, on Shabbat and Festivals, when we have less to worry about, we can pray with even greater devotion.

The first thing that is essential is at least to know the meaning and translation of the words of the prayers. If one cannot concentrate every day on the entire prayers, it would be a good idea one day to concentrate on one part, the next day on the next part, so that in the course of a week one will have concentrated on all the prayers. Or to make Shabbat the special day on which to work through the prayers.

To get you started, we have provided brief explanations for the prayers for the Friday evening services and included English transliterations to assist those to whom the Hebrew language is not yet familiar to pray along in the original Hebrew.

Please note: Since one of the prohibited actions on the Shabbat is carrying items from a private domain into a public one, and vice versa, make sure to bring this book to the synagogue before the onset of Shabbat. Alternatively, you can use it before the Shabbat as a study guide.

Blessings for Shabbat & Festival Candle Lighting

Lighting Shabbat and festival candles is the historic responsibility and privilege of every Jewish wife and mother. It is this 3,700 year-old tradition which Jewish women remember and observe in welcoming the "Shabbat Queen" or the Festival. It is this mitzvah that rekindles the Divine spark in every Jewish being.

The candles are lit at least 18 minutes before sunset on Friday or on the first Festival evening, and—using a flame source that was kindled before the onset of the Festival or Shabbat—45 minutes after sunset on the second night of a Festival, and when a Festival starts on Saturday night.

Married women kindle two candles, adding an additional candle for each member of their household. As soon as one's daughter is old enough to recite the blessing (approximately 2-3 years old), she should kindle her own Shabbat candle as well. Children should light before their mother in case they need assistance.

It is customary to place a few coins in a charity box prior to lighting the candles (except when lighting on the second night of a Festival or when the Festival starts on Saturday night (when the handling of money is forbidden)).

The time of lighting is considered especially propitious for praying for oneself and one's family.

Blessings for Shabbat and Festival Candle Lighting

At the appropriate time (see your local Jewish calendar) light the candles (girls light one candle and married women kindle two, adding one for each child). Draw your hands three times around the candles and toward your face. Cover your eyes with your hands, and recite the appropriate blessing.

On Friday Evening

בָּרוּךְ אַתָּה יְיָ, אֱלֹהֵינוּ מֶלֶךְ הָעוֹלָם, אֲשֶׁר קִדְּשָׁנוּ בְּמִצְוֹתָיו, וְצִוָּנוּ לְהַדְלִיק נֵר שֶׁל שַׁבָּת קֹדֶשׁ:

Böruch atöh adonöy, elohaynu melech hö-olöm, asher kid'shönu b'mitzvosöv, v'tzivönu l'hadlik nayr shel shabös kodesh.

Blessed are You, Lord our God, King of the universe, Who has sanctified us with His commandments, and commanded us to kindle the light of the holy Shabbat.

On the Eve of Passover, Shavuot and Sukkot

בָּרוּךְ אַתָּה יְיָ, אֱלֹהֵינוּ מֶלֶךְ הָעוֹלָם, אֲשֶׁר קִדְּשָׁנוּ בְּמִצְוֹתָיו, וְצִוָּנוּ לְהַדְלִיק נֵר שֶׁל יוֹם טוֹב:

Böruch atöh adonöy, elohaynu melech hö-olöm, asher kid'shönu b'mitzvosöv, v'tzivönu l'hadlik nayr shel yom tov.

Blessed are You, Lord our God, King of the universe, Who has sanctified us with His commandments, and commanded us to kindle the Yom Tov light.

Continue with the belssing on the following page.
(Except on the last two nights of Passover.)

41

בָּרוּךְ אַתָּה יְיָ,
אֱלֹהֵינוּ מֶלֶךְ הָעוֹלָם,
שֶׁהֶחֱיָנוּ וְקִיְּמָנוּ
וְהִגִּיעָנוּ לִזְמַן הַזֶּה:

Böruch atöh adonöy,
elohaynu melech hö-olöm,
she-heche-yönu v'kiy'mönu
v'higi-önu liz'man ha-zeh.

Blessed are You, Lord our God, King of the universe, Who has granted us life, sustained us and enabled us to reach this occasion.

On the Eve of Shabbat and Festivals

בָּרוּךְ אַתָּה יְיָ, אֱלֹהֵינוּ
מֶלֶךְ הָעוֹלָם, אֲשֶׁר קִדְּשָׁנוּ
בְּמִצְוֹתָיו, וְצִוָּנוּ לְהַדְלִיק
נֵר שֶׁל שַׁבָּת וְשֶׁל יוֹם טוֹב:

Böruch atöh adonöy, elohaynu
melech hö-olöm, asher kid'shönu
b'mitzvosöv, v'tzivönu l'hadlik
nayr shel shabos v'shel yom tov.

Blessed are You, Lord our God, King of the universe, Who has sanctified us with His commandments, and commanded us to kindle the Shabbat and Yom Tov light.

Continue with the blessing below:
(Except on the last two nights of Passover.)

בָּרוּךְ אַתָּה יְיָ,
אֱלֹהֵינוּ מֶלֶךְ הָעוֹלָם,
שֶׁהֶחֱיָנוּ וְקִיְּמָנוּ
וְהִגִּיעָנוּ לִזְמַן הַזֶּה:

Böruch atöh adonöy,
elohaynu melech hö-olöm,
she-heche-yönu v'kiy'mönu
v'higi-önu liz'man ha-zeh.

Blessed are You, Lord our God, King of the universe, Who has granted us life, sustained us and enabled us to reach this occasion.

Q&A About Candle Lighting

Q: What is the significance of the Shabbat and Festival candle lighting?

A: These are days of spiritual light and we introduce them by kindling material light in this world.

Q: It is past 18 minutes to sunset on Friday afternoon, what should I do?

A: If it is still before sunset, you should light the candles, but if it is past sunset, you should not light the candles. (Check your local Jewish calendar for the proper candle lighting times.)

Q: Why are the hands drawn around the candles and toward the face?

A: This symbolizes our beckoning in of the Shabbat, bringing to our eyes and introducing into our heart the lights of the Shabbat candles.

Q: Can men light the Shabbat candles?

A: If there are no women in the household who are lighting the candles, then men should light the candles (following the same procedure).

43

"Yedid Nefesh"

It is customary to say this hymn before praying the Friday evening service.

Y'did nefesh öv höra-chamön,
m'shoch av-d'chö el r'tzonechö,
yörutz av-d'chö k'mo ayöl,
yishta-chaveh el mul ha-dörechö,
ye-erav lo y'dido-sechö, mi-nofes
tzuf v'chöl tö-am.

יְדִיד נֶפֶשׁ אָב הָרַחֲמָן,
מְשׁוֹךְ עַבְדְּךָ אֶל רְצוֹנֶךָ,
יָרוּץ עַבְדְּךָ כְּמוֹ אַיָּל,
יִשְׁתַּחֲוֶה אֶל מוּל הֲדָרֶךָ,
יֶעֱרַב לוֹ יְדִידוֹתֶיךָ, מִנֹּפֶת
צוּף וְכָל טָעַם :

Hödur nö-eh ziv hö-olöm, nafshi
cholas ahavö-sechö, önö ayl nö r'fö
nö löh, b'har-os löh no-am zivechö,
öz tis-chazayk v'sis-rapay, v'hö-y'söh
löh sim-chas olöm.

הָדוּר נָאֶה זִיו הָעוֹלָם, נַפְשִׁי
חוֹלַת אַהֲבָתֶךָ, אָנָּא אֵל נָא רְפָא
נָא לָהּ, בְּהַרְאוֹת לָהּ נוֹעַם זִיוֶךָ,
אָז תִּתְחַזֵּק וְתִתְרַפֵּא, וְהָיְתָה
לָהּ שִׂמְחַת עוֹלָם :

Vösik ye-hemu racha-mechö, v'chusö
nö al bayn ahu-vechö, ki zeh kamöh
nich-sof nich-safti lir-os b'sif-eres
uzechö, ay-leh chö-m'döh libi
v'chusöh nö v'al tis-alöm.

וָתִיק יֶהֱמוּ רַחֲמֶיךָ, וְחוּסָה
נָא עַל בֵּן אֲהוּבֶךָ, כִּי זֶה כַּמָּה
נִכְסוֹף נִכְסַפְתִּי לִרְאוֹת בְּתִפְאֶרֶת
עֻזֶךָ, אֵלֶּה חָמְדָה לִבִּי
וְחוּסָה נָא וְאַל תִּתְעַלָּם :

"Yedid Nefesh"

הִגָּלֵה נָא וּפְרוֹס חֲבִיבִי עָלַי אֶת
סֻכַּת שְׁלוֹמֶךָ, תָּאִיר אֶרֶץ
מִכְּבוֹדֶךָ, נָגִילָה וְנִשְׂמְחָה
בָּךְ, מַהֵר אָהוּב כִּי בָא מוֹעֵד,
וְחָנֵּנוּ כִּימֵי עוֹלָם:

Higö-leh nö uf'ros chavivi ölai es
sukas sh'lomechö, tö-ir eretz
mik'vodechö, nögilöh v'nis-m'chöh
böch, ma-hayr öhuv ki vö mo-ayd,
v'chönaynu kimay olöm.

Beloved of [my] soul, merciful Father, draw Your servant to Your will. [Then] Your servant will run as swiftly as a deer; he will bow before Your splendor; Your acts of affection will be sweeter than honeycomb and every pleasant taste. Glorious, resplendent One, Light of the world, my soul is lovesick for You; I beseech You, O God, pray heal it by showing it the sweetness of Your splendor. Then it will be strengthened and healed and will experience everlasting joy. O pious One, may Your mercy be aroused and have compassion upon Your beloved child. For it is long that I have been yearning to behold the glory of Your majesty. These my heart desires, so have pity and do not conceal Yourself. Reveal Yourself, my Beloved, and spread over me the shelter of Your peace. Let the earth be illuminated by Your glory; we will rejoice and exult in You. Hasten, Beloved, for the time has come; and be gracious unto us as in days of yore.

45

Overview of
The Friday Evening Service

The "*Kabbalat Shabbat*" ([prayer for] welcoming the Shabbat) begins with six psalms: 95-99 and 29. The custom of reciting these psalms is relatively new. In ancient days the Shabbat was welcomed in a special way just before sunset. From the Talmud we learn, for example, that Rabbi Chanina used to put on his best clothes and say, "Come, let us go forth and welcome the Shabbat Queen." No doubt some appropriate psalms were recited on this occasion.

The custom of beginning the service with the six psalms mentioned above, followed by the hymn of *Lecha Dodi*, however, is actually only about 400 years old. It was introduced by the great Kabbalist Rabbi Moshe Cordovero (1522-1570) of Safed (brother-in-law of Rabbi Shlomo Halevi Alkabetz, author of Lecha Dodi), and has been held by both Sefardi and Ashkenazi Jews ever since.

The six psalms represent the Six Days of Creation which preceded the holy Shabbat day of rest. They are hymns of praise to God, which serve to inspire us and put us in the right frame of mind for welcoming the Shabbat Queen.

It has been noted that the *Rashei Tayvot* (the first letters of the initial words) of these psalms add up to 430, the numerical value of the

Hebrew word נפש (soul), significant of the soulful inspiration that these psalms bring us on the eve of Shabbat. Taking a closer look at these psalms, we can distinguish three main themes that run through all of them.

One is the spirit of joy and exultation that permeates these psalms. It sets our mood for our welcoming the Shabbat with true joy, as one of the greatest gifts that God gave the Jewish people.

The second theme that is common to all these psalms is that of Creation, for Shabbat is the "crown" of God's creative work. This theme calls forth in us our acknowledgment of God's majesty and our willing submission to His kingship. Many verses in these psalms express such sentiments in various ways.

The third theme is the anticipation of the Messianic Era and the new order that will transform this world into what is generally called *Olam Haba*, the World to Come; at that time our material world will attain the ultimate perfection for which it is destined and God's supreme majesty will be acknowledged by all the nations of the world. That new world is due to become a reality in the seventh millennium, which is appropriately called "Shabbat." The preceding six thousand years of mankind's history compare to the six days of the week in relation to Shabbat.

This is particularly true of the present millennium (the sixth). It is like *"Erev Shabbat"* the eve of Shabbat, when the final preparations for Shabbat must be made. With this in mind, our Sages observed, "He who prepares for Shabbat on Erev Shabbat, has food for Shabbat, but he who does not prepare for Shabbat, what will he eat on Shabbat?" The "food"

they speak of is the Torah and *mitzvot*, the real food of our souls. This is the time to prepare ourselves for the period that is called the "Eternal Shabbat," through the most dedicated adherence to the Torah and *mitzvot* in daily life, so as to fully enjoy the great rewards of the Eternal Shabbat. Indeed, Shabbat itself has some of the quality of *Olam Haba* (the World to Come).

After the *Kabbalat Shabbat* prayers we proceed with the regular Evening service and substitue a special *Amidah* (silent prayer) for Shabbat or Festivals. The Evening service is concluded by special concluding prayers for the Shabbat or Festival.

The "Kabbalat Shabbat"

Prayer for Welcoming the Shabbat

The Friday evening service begins here. When a Festival or *Chol HaMoed* (intermediate days of a festival) falls on Shabbat, omit the following and begin with *Mizmor L'dovid*, on page 58.

Come, Let Us Sing...   ...לְכוּ נְרַנְּנָה

In this first Psalm of the service we find Adam's first words after God breathed into him the Breath of Life: *"Come, let us prostrate ourselves and bow down; let us bend the knee before the Lord our Maker."* He called to all creatures of the world to acknowledge the Creator and to submit to His will. The Psalm also notes the special relationship we have with God, how we are His people and He looks after us as a shepherd tends to his flock. It concludes with the miraculous exodus from Egypt, where God first showed His personal concern for our people.

L'chu n'ran'nöh la-donöy, nöri-öh
l'tzur yish-aynu. N'kad'möh fönöv
b'sodöh, biz'miros nöri-a lo.
Ki ayl gödol adonöy, umelech
gödol al köl elohim. Asher
b'yödo mech-k'ray öretz, v'so-afos
hörim lo. Asher lo ha-yöm v'hu

לְכוּ נְרַנְּנָה לַיָי, נָרִיעָה
לְצוּר יִשְׁעֵנוּ: נְקַדְּמָה פָנָיו
בְּתוֹדָה, בִּזְמִרוֹת נָרִיעַ לוֹ:
כִּי אֵל גָּדוֹל יְיָ, וּמֶלֶךְ
גָּדוֹל עַל כָּל אֱלֹהִים: אֲשֶׁר
בְּיָדוֹ מֶחְקְרֵי אָרֶץ, וְתוֹעֲפוֹת
הָרִים לוֹ: אֲשֶׁר לוֹ הַיָּם וְהוּא

49

ösöhu, v'yabeshes yödöv yö-tzöru.	עָשָׂהוּ, וְיַבֶּשֶׁת יָדָיו יָצָרוּ:
Bo-u nish-tachaveh v'nichrö-öh,	בֹּאוּ נִשְׁתַּחֲוֶה וְנִכְרָעָה,
niv-r'chöh lif'nay adonöy osaynu.	נִבְרְכָה לִפְנֵי יְיָ עֹשֵׂנוּ:
Ki hu elohaynu va-anachnu am	כִּי הוּא אֱלֹהֵינוּ וַאֲנַחְנוּ עַם
mar-iso v'tzon yödo, ha-yom im	מַרְעִיתוֹ וְצֹאן יָדוֹ, הַיּוֹם אִם
b'kolo sishmö-u. Al tak-shu	בְּקֹלוֹ תִשְׁמָעוּ: אַל תַּקְשׁוּ
l'vav'chem kim'rivöh, k'yom masö	לְבַבְכֶם כִּמְרִיבָה, כְּיוֹם מַסָּה
ba-midbör. Asher nisuni avosaychem,	בַּמִּדְבָּר: אֲשֶׁר נִסּוּנִי אֲבוֹתֵיכֶם,
b'chönuni, gam rö-u fö-öli. Arbö-im	בְּחָנוּנִי, גַּם רָאוּ פָעֳלִי: אַרְבָּעִים
shönöh ökut b'dor, vö-omar am	שָׁנָה אָקוּט בְּדוֹר, וָאֹמַר עַם
to-ay layvöv haym v'haym lo yöd'u	תֹּעֵי לֵבָב הֵם וְהֵם לֹא יָדְעוּ
d'röchöy. Asher nishba-ti v'api,	דְרָכָי: אֲשֶׁר נִשְׁבַּעְתִּי בְאַפִּי,
im y'vo-un el m'nuchösi.	אִם יְבֹאוּן אֶל מְנוּחָתִי:

Come, let us sing to the Lord; let us raise our voices in jubilation to the Rock of our deliverance. Let us approach Him with thanksgiving; let us raise our voices to Him in song. For the Lord is a great God, and a great King over all supernal beings; in His hands are the depths of the earth, and the heights of the mountains are His. Indeed, the sea is His, for He made it; His hands formed the dry land. Come, let us prostrate ourselves and bow down; let us bend the knee before the Lord our Maker. For He is our God, and we are the people that He tends, the flock under His [guiding] hand — even this very day, if you would but hearken to His voice! Do not harden your heart as at Merivah, as on the day at Massah in the wilderness, where your fathers tested Me; they tried Me, though they had seen My deeds. For forty years I quarreled with that

generation; and I said, they are a people of erring hearts, they do not know My ways. So I vowed in My anger that they shall not enter My resting place.

Sing to the Lord...

שִׁירוּ לַיָי ...

This Psalm too begins with a call to sing God's praises. It speaks of the Messianic Era, when the extraordinary salvation that God will bring to our people will call for a new kind of praise. The revelation of God's majesty in those future days will cause all mankind to worship God with a sense of holiness and awe.

שִׁירוּ לַיָי שִׁיר חָדָשׁ,
שִׁירוּ לַיָי כָּל הָאָרֶץ :
שִׁירוּ לַיָי בָּרְכוּ שְׁמוֹ, בַּשְּׂרוּ
מִיּוֹם לְיוֹם יְשׁוּעָתוֹ :
סַפְּרוּ בַגּוֹיִם כְּבוֹדוֹ, בְּכָל
הָעַמִּים נִפְלְאוֹתָיו : כִּי גָדוֹל יְיָ
וּמְהֻלָּל מְאֹד, נוֹרָא הוּא עַל כָּל
אֱלֹהִים : כִּי כָּל אֱלֹהֵי הָעַמִּים
אֱלִילִים, וַיָי שָׁמַיִם עָשָׂה :
הוֹד וְהָדָר לְפָנָיו, עֹז וְתִפְאֶרֶת
בְּמִקְדָּשׁוֹ : הָבוּ לַיָי
מִשְׁפְּחוֹת עַמִּים, הָבוּ לַיָי
כָּבוֹד וָעֹז : הָבוּ לַיָי כְּבוֹד
שְׁמוֹ, שְׂאוּ מִנְחָה וּבֹאוּ

Shiru la-donöy shir chödösh,
shiru la-donöy köl hö-öretz.
Shiru ladonöy bö-r'chu sh'mo, bas'ru
mi-yom l'yom y'shu-öso.
Sap'ru vago-yim k'vodo, b'chöl
hö-amim nif-l'osöv. Ki gödol adonöy
um'hulöl m'od, norö hu al köl
elohim. Ki köl elohay hö-amim
elilim, vadonöy shöma-yim ösöh.
Hod v'hödör l'fönöv, oz v'sif-eres
b'mik-dösho. Hövu ladonöy
mish-p'chos amim, hövu ladonöy
kövod vö-oz. Hövu la-donöy k'vod
sh'mo, s'u min-chöh uvo-u

51

l'chatz'rosöv. Hish-tachavu ladonöy
b'had'ras kodesh, chilu mipönöv köl
hö-öretz. Im'ru vago-yim adonöy
möloch, af tikon tayvayl bal timot,
yödin amim b'mayshörim.
Yis-m'chu ha-shöma-yim v'sögayl
hö-öretz, yir-am hayöm um'lo-o.
Ya-aloz södai v'chöl asher bo, öz
y'ran'nu köl atzay yö-ar.
Lif'nay adonöy ki vö, ki vö
lishpot hö-öretz, yishpot tayvayl
b'tzedek, v'amim be-emunöso.

לְחַצְרוֹתָיו : הִשְׁתַּחֲווּ לַיְיָ
בְּהַדְרַת קֹדֶשׁ, חִילוּ מִפָּנָיו כָּל
הָאָרֶץ : אִמְרוּ בַגּוֹיִם יְיָ
מָלָךְ, אַף תִּכּוֹן תֵּבֵל בַּל תִּמּוֹט,
יָדִין עַמִּים בְּמֵישָׁרִים :
יִשְׂמְחוּ הַשָּׁמַיִם וְתָגֵל
הָאָרֶץ, יִרְעַם הַיָּם וּמְלֹאוֹ :
יַעֲלֹז שָׂדַי וְכָל אֲשֶׁר בּוֹ, אָז
יְרַנְּנוּ כָּל עֲצֵי יָעַר :
לִפְנֵי יְיָ כִּי בָא, כִּי בָא
לִשְׁפֹּט הָאָרֶץ, יִשְׁפֹּט תֵּבֵל
בְּצֶדֶק, וְעַמִּים בֶּאֱמוּנָתוֹ :

*Sing to the Lord a new song; sing to the Lord, all the earth. Sing to the Lord,
bless His Name; proclaim His deliverance from day to day. Recount His glory
among the nations, His wonders among all the peoples. For the Lord is great
and highly praised; He is awesome above all gods. For all the gods of the
nations are naught, but the Lord made the heavens. Majesty and splendor are
before Him, might and beauty in His Sanctuary. Render to the Lord, O
families of nations, render to the Lord honor and might. Render to the Lord the
honor due to His Name; bring an offering and come to His courtyards. Bow
down to the Lord in resplendent holiness; tremble before Him, all the earth.
Proclaim among the nations: "The Lord reigns"; indeed, the world is firmly
established that it shall not falter; He will judge the people with righteousness.
The heavens will rejoice, the earth will exult; the sea and its fullness will roar.
The fields and everything therein will jubilate; then all the trees of the forest*

will sing. Before the Lord [they shall rejoice] for He has come, for He has come to judge the earth; He will judge the world with justice, and the nations with His truth.

When the Lord...

יְיָ מָלָךְ ...

This Psalm continues the theme of the Messianic Era. At that time it will be an occasion for tremendous rejoicing, for the world will then enter the era of its fulfillment and perfection. While God himself will still be hidden from man — as if he were surrounded by a cloud and by darkness — nevertheless, His reign on earth will be clearly recognized by all. The words 'Light is sown for the righteous' bear significant meaning. The good works that a person does are likend to the sowing or planting of seeds. The 'light' sown refers to the Torah and its commandments. Since the Torah is God's thought and knowledge, it is attached to the infinite. Thus when we perform a mitzvah, commandment, though the event may be transient, the effects are enduring and benefit us forever.

Adonöy möloch tögayl hö-öretz, yis-m'chu i-yim rabim. Önön va-aröfel s'vivöv, tzedek umishpöt m'chon kis'o. Aysh l'fönöv tay-laych. us'la-hayt söviv tzöröv. Hay-iru v'rököv tayvayl, rö-asöh va-töchel hö-öretz. Hörim kadonag nömasu milif'nay adonöy, milif'nay adon köl hö-öretz. Higidu ha-shöma-yim

יְיָ מָלָךְ תָּגֵל הָאָרֶץ,
יִשְׂמְחוּ אִיִּים רַבִּים: עָנָן וַעֲרָפֶל
סְבִיבָיו, צֶדֶק וּמִשְׁפָּט מְכוֹן
כִּסְאוֹ: אֵשׁ לְפָנָיו תֵּלֵךְ,
וּתְלַהֵט סָבִיב צָרָיו: הֵאִירוּ
בְרָקָיו תֵּבֵל, רָאֲתָה וַתָּחֵל
הָאָרֶץ: הָרִים כַּדּוֹנַג נָמַסּוּ
מִלִּפְנֵי יְיָ, מִלִּפְנֵי אֲדוֹן כָּל
הָאָרֶץ: הִגִּידוּ הַשָּׁמַיִם

53

tzidko, v'rö-u chöl hö-amim
k'vodo. Yay-voshu köl ov'day fesel
ha-mis-hal'lim bö-elilim, hish-tachavu
lo köl elohim. Shöm'öh va-tismach
tziyon, vatö-gaylnö b'nos y'hudöh,
l'ma-an mishpötechö adonöy. Ki atöh
adonöy elyon al köl hö-öretz, m'od
na-alaysö al köl elohim. O-havay
adonöy sin'u rö, shomayr naf'shos
chasidöv, mi-yad r'shö-im ya-tzilaym.
Or zöru-a la-tzadik, ul'yish'ray layv
simchöh. Sim'chu tzadikim badonöy,
v'hodu l'zaycher köd-sho.

צִדְקוֹ, וְרָאוּ כָל הָעַמִּים
כְּבוֹדוֹ: יֵבֹשׁוּ כָּל עֹבְדֵי פֶסֶל
הַמִּתְהַלְלִים בָּאֱלִילִים, הִשְׁתַּחֲווּ
לוֹ כָּל אֱלֹהִים: שָׁמְעָה וַתִּשְׂמַח
צִיּוֹן, וַתָּגֵלְנָה בְּנוֹת יְהוּדָה,
לְמַעַן מִשְׁפָּטֶיךָ יְיָ: כִּי אַתָּה
יְיָ עֶלְיוֹן עַל כָּל הָאָרֶץ, מְאֹד
נַעֲלֵיתָ עַל כָּל אֱלֹהִים: אֹהֲבֵי
יְיָ שִׂנְאוּ רָע, שֹׁמֵר נַפְשׁוֹת
חֲסִידָיו, מִיַּד רְשָׁעִים יַצִּילֵם:
אוֹר זָרֻעַ לַצַּדִּיק, וּלְיִשְׁרֵי לֵב
שִׂמְחָה: שִׂמְחוּ צַדִּיקִים בַּיְיָ,
וְהוֹדוּ לְזֵכֶר קָדְשׁוֹ:

When the Lord will reveal His kingship, the earth will exult; the multitudes of islands will rejoice. Clouds and dense darkness will surround Him; justice and mercy will be the foundation of His throne. Fire will go before Him and consume His foes all around. His lightnings will illuminate the world; the earth will see and tremble. The mountains will melt like wax before the Lord, before the Master of all the earth. The heavens will declare His justice, and all the nations will behold His glory. All who worship graven images, who take pride in idols, will be ashamed; all idol worshippers will prostrate themselves before Him. Zion will hear and rejoice, the towns of Judah will exult, because of Your judgments, O Lord. For You, Lord, transcend all the earth; You are exceedingly exalted above all the supernal beings. You who love the Lord, hate evil; He watches over the souls of His pious ones, He saves them from the hand

of the wicked. Light is sown for the righteous, and joy for the upright in heart. Rejoice in the Lord, you righteous, and extol His holy Name.

A Psalm. Sing...

מִזְמוֹר, שִׁירוּ...

This Psalm speaks of the Messianic Era. King David acclaims God's wondrous acts when the time will come to reveal His might and glory. During the long and dark exile the nations of the world mocked and derided the Jewish people, saying that God has forgotten and forsaken them, and they could be persecuted without fear of punishment. But those wicked nations are due to find out how wrong they were, as we note here in this Psalm.

מִזְמוֹר, שִׁירוּ לַיְיָ שִׁיר חָדָשׁ,
כִּי נִפְלָאוֹת עָשָׂה, הוֹשִׁיעָה לּוֹ
יְמִינוֹ וּזְרוֹעַ קָדְשׁוֹ: הוֹדִיעַ
יְיָ יְשׁוּעָתוֹ, לְעֵינֵי הַגּוֹיִם
גִּלָּה צִדְקָתוֹ: זָכַר חַסְדּוֹ
וֶאֱמוּנָתוֹ לְבֵית יִשְׂרָאֵל, רָאוּ
כָל אַפְסֵי אָרֶץ, אֵת יְשׁוּעַת
אֱלֹהֵינוּ: הָרִיעוּ לַיְיָ כָּל
הָאָרֶץ, פִּצְחוּ וְרַנְּנוּ וְזַמֵּרוּ:
זַמְּרוּ לַיְיָ בְּכִנּוֹר, בְּכִנּוֹר
וְקוֹל זִמְרָה: בַּחֲצֹצְרוֹת וְקוֹל
שׁוֹפָר, הָרִיעוּ לִפְנֵי הַמֶּלֶךְ
יְיָ: יִרְעַם הַיָּם וּמְלֹאוֹ,

Mizmor, shiru ladonöy shir chödösh, ki niflö-os ösöh, hoshi-öh lo y'mino uz'roa köd-sho. Hodi-a adonöy y'shu-öso, l'aynay ha-go-yim gilöh tzid'koso. Zöchar chasdo ve-emunöso l'vays yisrö-ayl, rö-u chöl af'say öretz, ays y'shu-as elohaynu. Höri-u ladonöy köl hö-öretz, pitz'chu v'ran'nu v'zamayru. Zam'ru ladonöy b'chi-nor, b'chi-nor v'kol zimröh. Ba-chatzo-tz'ros v'kol shoför, höri-u lif'nay ha-melech adonöy. Yir-am ha-yöm um'lo-o,

tay-vayl v'yosh'vay vöh. N'höros   תֵּבֵל וְיֹשְׁבֵי בָהּ: נְהָרוֹת

yimcha-u chöf, yachad hörim   יִמְחֲאוּ כָף, יַחַד הָרִים

y'ranaynu. Lif'nay adonöy ki vö   יְרַנֵּנוּ: לִפְנֵי יְיָ כִּי בָא

lish-pot hö-öretz, yish-pot tayvayl   לִשְׁפֹּט הָאָרֶץ, יִשְׁפֹּט תֵּבֵל

b'tzedek, v'amim b'mayshörim.   בְּצֶדֶק, וְעַמִּים בְּמֵישָׁרִים:

A Psalm. Sing to the Lord a new song, for He has performed wonders; His right hand and holy arm have wrought deliverance for Him. The Lord has made known His salvation; He has revealed His justice before the eyes of the nations. He has remembered His loving-kindness and faithfulness to the House of Israel; all, from the farthest corners of the earth, witnessed the deliverance by our God. Raise your voices in jubilation to the Lord, all the earth; burst into joyous song and chanting. Sing to the Lord with a harp, with a harp and the sound of song. With trumpets and the sound of the shofar, jubilate before the King, the Lord. The sea and its fullness will roar in joy, the earth and its inhabitants. The rivers will clap their hands, the mountains will sing together. [They will rejoice] before the Lord, for He has come to judge the earth; He will judge the world with justice, and the nations with righteousness.

When the Lord...   ...יְיָ מָלָךְ

Speaking of God's holiness and the laws of justice and morality which He has established, King David recalls Moses, Aaron, and Samuel to indicate that it was thanks to such leaders that the Jewish people were able to maintain their high standards of morality and justice. We are reminded that the leaders and all the Jewish people are responsible to the

same set of laws. Each and every Jew is equally obligated to fulfill the commandments of the Torah, regardless of his spiritual or political post.

Adonöy mölöch yir-g'zu amim,	יְיָ מָלָךְ יִרְגְּזוּ עַמִּים,
yoshayv k'ruvim tönut hö-öretz.	יֹשֵׁב כְּרוּבִים תָּנוּט הָאָרֶץ :
Adonöy b'tziyon gödol, v'röm hu al	יְיָ בְּצִיּוֹן גָּדוֹל, וְרָם הוּא עַל
köl hö-amim. Yodu shim'cho gödol	כָּל הָעַמִּים : יוֹדוּ שִׁמְךָ גָּדוֹל
v'norö, ködosh hu. V'oz melech	וְנוֹרָא, קָדוֹשׁ הוּא : וְעֹז מֶלֶךְ
mish-pöt öhayv, atöh ko-nantö	מִשְׁפָּט אָהֵב, אַתָּה כּוֹנַנְתָּ
may-shörim, mish-pöt utz'dököh	מֵישָׁרִים, מִשְׁפָּט וּצְדָקָה
b'ya-akov atöh ösisö. Rom'mu adonöy	בְּיַעֲקֹב אַתָּה עָשִׂיתָ : רוֹמְמוּ יְיָ
elohaynu v'hishta-chavu la-hadom	אֱלֹהֵינוּ וְהִשְׁתַּחֲווּ לַהֲדֹם
rag-löv, ködosh hu. Mosheh	רַגְלָיו, קָדוֹשׁ הוּא : מֹשֶׁה
V'aharon b'cho-hanöv ush'mu-ayl	וְאַהֲרֹן בְּכֹהֲנָיו וּשְׁמוּאֵל
b'kor'ay sh'mo, kor-im el adonöy	בְּקֹרְאֵי שְׁמוֹ, קֹרִאים אֶל יְיָ
v'hu ya-anaym. B'amud önön	וְהוּא יַעֲנֵם : בְּעַמּוּד עָנָן
y'dabayr alayhem, shöm'ru	יְדַבֵּר אֲלֵיהֶם, שָׁמְרוּ
aydosöv v'chok nösan lömo. Adonöy	עֵדֹתָיו וְחֹק נָתַן לָמוֹ : יְיָ
elohaynu atöh anisöm, ayl nosay	אֱלֹהֵינוּ אַתָּה עֲנִיתָם, אֵל נֹשֵׂא
hö-yisö lö-hem, v'nokaym al	הָיִיתָ לָהֶם, וְנֹקֵם עַל
ali-losöm. Rom'mu adonöy elohaynu	עֲלִילוֹתָם : רוֹמְמוּ יְיָ אֱלֹהֵינוּ
v'hishta-chavu l'har köd-sho,	וְהִשְׁתַּחֲווּ לְהַר קָדְשׁוֹ,
ki ködosh adonöy elohaynu.	כִּי קָדוֹשׁ יְיָ אֱלֹהֵינוּ :

When the Lord will reveal His kingship, the nations will tremble; the earth will quake before Him who is enthroned upon the kruvim, [before] the Lord who is

in Zion, who is great and exalted above all the peoples. They will extol Your Name which is great, awesome and holy. And [they will praise] the might of the King who loves justice. You have established uprightness; You have made [the laws of] justice and righteousness in Jacob. Exalt the Lord our God, and bow down at His footstool; He is holy. Moses and Aaron among His priests, and Samuel among those who invoke His Name, would call upon the Lord and He would answer them. He would speak to them from a pillar of cloud; they observed His testimonies and the decrees which He gave them. Lord our God, You have answered them; You were a forgiving God for their sake, yet bringing retribution for their own misdeeds. Exalt the Lord our God, and bow down at His holy mountain, for the Lord our God is holy.

A Psalm by David...   מִזְמוֹר לְדָוִד...

Recited Standing

This Psalm contains God's name 18 times, which is significant since it is the same as the numerical value of the Hebrew word Chai, Life.

The seven repetitions of the words 'Kol Hashem' (Voice of the Lord), in this Psalm correspond to the seven days of Creation, when everything was created by God's word. In the kabbalah (Jewish mysticism) we are told that a far-reaching and tremendous effect takes place in the Upper worlds when this Psalm is recited with concentration and joy.

Mizmor l'dövid, hövu la-donöy b'nay
aylim, hövu la-donöy kövod vö-oz.
Hövu la-donöy k'vod sh'mo,
hishtachavu la-donöy b'had'ras
kodesh. Kol adonöy al ha-mö-yim,
ayl ha-kövod hir-im, adonöy al
ma-yim rabim. Kol adonöy bako-ach,
kol adonöy be-hödör. Kol adonöy
shovayr arözim, va-y'shabayr adonöy
es ar'zay ha-l'vönon. Va-yarkidaym
k'mo aygel, l'vönon v'siryon k'mo
ven r'aymim. Kol adonöy cho-tzayv
la-havos aysh. Kol adonöy yöchil
midbör, yöchil adonöy midbar
ködaysh. Kol adonöy y'cholayl
a-yölos va-yechesof y'öros,
uv'haychölo, kulo omayr kövod.
Adonöy la-mabul yöshöv, va-yayshev
adonöy melech l'olöm. Adonöy oz
l'amo yitayn, adonöy y'vöraych
es amo va-shölom.

מִזְמוֹר לְדָוִד, הָבוּ לַיְיָ בְּנֵי
אֵלִים, הָבוּ לַיְיָ כָּבוֹד וָעֹז :
הָבוּ לַיְיָ כְּבוֹד שְׁמוֹ,
הִשְׁתַּחֲווּ לַיְיָ בְּהַדְרַת
קֹדֶשׁ : קוֹל יְיָ עַל הַמָּיִם,
אֵל הַכָּבוֹד הִרְעִים, יְיָ עַל
מַיִם רַבִּים : קוֹל יְיָ בַּכֹּחַ,
קוֹל יְיָ בֶּהָדָר : קוֹל יְיָ
שֹׁבֵר אֲרָזִים, וַיְשַׁבֵּר יְיָ
אֶת אַרְזֵי הַלְּבָנוֹן : וַיַּרְקִידֵם
כְּמוֹ עֵגֶל, לְבָנוֹן וְשִׂרְיוֹן כְּמוֹ
בֶן רְאֵמִים : קוֹל יְיָ חֹצֵב
לַהֲבוֹת אֵשׁ : קוֹל יְיָ יָחִיל
מִדְבָּר, יָחִיל יְיָ מִדְבַּר
קָדֵשׁ : קוֹל יְיָ יְחוֹלֵל
אַיָּלוֹת וַיֶּחֱשֹׂף יְעָרוֹת,
וּבְהֵיכָלוֹ, כֻּלּוֹ אֹמֵר כָּבוֹד :
יְיָ לַמַּבּוּל יָשָׁב, וַיֵּשֶׁב
יְיָ מֶלֶךְ לְעוֹלָם : יְיָ עֹז
לְעַמּוֹ יִתֵּן, יְיָ יְבָרֵךְ
אֶת עַמּוֹ בַשָּׁלוֹם :

*A Psalm by David. Render to the Lord, children of the mighty, render to the
Lord honor and strength. Render to the Lord the honor due to His Name; bow
down to the Lord in resplendent holiness. The voice of the Lord is over the*

waters, the God of glory thunders; the Lord is over mighty waters. The voice of the Lord resounds with might; the voice of the Lord resounds with majesty. The voice of the Lord breaks cedars; the Lord shatters the cedars of Lebanon. He makes them leap like a calf; Lebanon and Sirion like a young wild ox. The voice of the Lord strikes flames of fire. The voice of the Lord makes the desert tremble; the Lord causes the desert of Kadesh to tremble. The voice of the Lord causes the does to calve, and strips the forests bare; and in His Sanctuary all proclaim His glory. The Lord sat [as King] at the Flood; the Lord will sit as King forever. The Lord will give strength to His people; the Lord will bless His people with peace.

We Implore You... אָנָּא, בְּכֹחַ...

Recited standing. It is customary to recite this paragraph silently.

This is a very holy and mystical prayer. In its original Hebrew form the prayer consists of 7 lines, each consisting of 6 words. The total number of words, 42, signify one of the mystical Divine names which has the same numerical value.

The 7 lines symbolize the 7 Divine Attributes (wisdom, kindness, severity, etc.) by means of which God rules the world. The number 6 also has a deep mystical meaning. It is related to the six wings of the angels Isaiah saw in his prophetic vision. The *Shema*, in its first verse in which we pronounce God's unity, also contains 6 words. While the average worshiper is not expected to delve into all the mysteries of the kaballah, everyone is expected to know, at least, the meaning of the words.

Önö, b'cho-ach g'dulas y'min'chö, **אָנָּא, בְּכֹחַ גְּדֻלַּת יְמִינְךָ,**
tatir tz'ruröh. Kabayl rinas am'chö, **תַּתִּיר צְרוּרָה: קַבֵּל רִנַּת עַמְּךָ,**
sag'vaynu, taharaynu, noröh. **שַׂגְּבֵנוּ, טַהֲרֵנוּ, נוֹרָא:**
Nö gibor, dor'shay yichud'chö, **נָא גִבּוֹר, דּוֹרְשֵׁי יִחוּדְךָ,**
k'vövas shöm'raym. Bö-r'chaym **כְּבָבַת שָׁמְרֵם: בָּרְכֵם**
taharaym, rachamay tzid'kös'chö **טַהֲרֵם, רַחֲמֵי צִדְקָתְךָ**
tömid göm'laym. Chasin ködosh, **תָּמִיד גָּמְלֵם: חֲסִין קָדוֹשׁ,**
b'rov tuv'chö nahayl adö-sechö. **בְּרוֹב טוּבְךָ נַהֵל עֲדָתֶךָ:**
Yöchid, gay-eh, l'am'chö p'nay, **יָחִיד, גֵּאֶה, לְעַמְּךָ פְּנֵה,**
zoch'ray k'dushösechö. Shav-ösaynu **זוֹכְרֵי קְדֻשָּׁתֶךָ: שַׁוְעָתֵנוּ**
kabayl, ush'ma tza-akösaynu, **קַבֵּל, וּשְׁמַע צַעֲקָתֵנוּ,**
yoday-a ta-alumos. Böruch shaym **יוֹדֵעַ תַּעֲלֻמוֹת: בָּרוּךְ שֵׁם**
k'vod mal'chuso l'olöm vö-ed. **כְּבוֹד מַלְכוּתוֹ לְעוֹלָם וָעֶד:**

We implore you, by the great power of Your right hand, release the captive. Accept the prayer of Your people; strengthen us, purify us, Awesome One. Mighty One, we beseech You, guard as the apple of the eye those who seek Your Oneness. Bless them, cleanse them; bestow upon them forever Your merciful righteousness. Powerful, Holy One, in Your abounding goodness, guide Your congregation. Only and Exalted One, turn to Your people who are mindful of Your holiness. Accept our supplication and hear our cry, You who know secret thoughts. Blessed be the name of the glory of His kingdom forever and ever.

Come, My Beloved... לְכָה דוֹדִי...

Recited standing

This beautiful hymn welcomes the Shabbat Queen. The refrain of this hymn *'Lecho Dodi'* and, indeed the entire motif of the hymn, in which the Shabbat is represented as a "Queen" whom we go out to welcome, is based on a Talmudic source, where we are told how two great Sages went out to welcome the Shabbat Queen in this fashion.

L'chöh dodi lik'ras kalöh,	לְכָה דוֹדִי לִקְרַאת כַּלָּה,
p'nay shabös n'kab'löh.	פְּנֵי שַׁבָּת נְקַבְּלָה :
L'chöh dodi lik'ras kalöh,	לְכָה דוֹדִי לִקְרַאת כַּלָּה,
p'nay shabös n'kab'löh.	פְּנֵי שַׁבָּת נְקַבְּלָה :

Come, my Beloved, to meet the Bride; let us welcome the Shabbat. Come, my Beloved, to meet the Bride; let us welcome the Shabbat.

Shömor v'zöchor b'dibur echöd,	שָׁמוֹר וְזָכוֹר בְּדִבּוּר אֶחָד,
hishmi-önu ayl ha-m'yuchöd,	הִשְׁמִיעָנוּ אֵל הַמְיֻחָד,
adonöy echöd ush'mo echöd,	יְיָ אֶחָד וּשְׁמוֹ אֶחָד,
l'shaym ul'sif-eres v'lis'hilöh.	לְשֵׁם וּלְתִפְאֶרֶת וְלִתְהִלָּה :
L'chöh dodi lik'ras kalöh,	לְכָה דוֹדִי לִקְרַאת כַּלָּה,
p'nay shabös n'kab'löh.	פְּנֵי שַׁבָּת נְקַבְּלָה :

"Observe" and "Remember," the one and only God caused us to hear in a

single utterance; the Lord is One and His name is One, for renown, for glory and for praise. Come, my Beloved, to meet the Bride; let us welcome the Shabbat.

Lik'ras shabös l'chu v'nayl'chöh,	לִקְרַאת שַׁבָּת לְכוּ וְנֵלְכָה,
ki hi m'kor ha-b'röchöh,	כִּי הִיא מְקוֹר הַבְּרָכָה,
may-rosh mikedem n'suchöh,	מֵרֹאשׁ מִקֶּדֶם נְסוּכָה,
sof ma-aseh b'ma-chashövöh t'chilöh.	סוֹף מַעֲשֶׂה בְּמַחֲשָׁבָה תְּחִלָּה :

L'chöh dodi lik'ras kalöh,	לְכָה דוֹדִי לִקְרַאת כַּלָּה,
p'nay shabös n'kab'löh.	פְּנֵי שַׁבָּת נְקַבְּלָה :

Come, let us go to welcome the Shabbat, for it is the source of blessing; from the beginning, from aforetime, it was chosen; last in creation, first in [God's] thought. Come, my Beloved, to meet the Bride; let us welcome the Shabbat.

Mikdash melech ir m'luchöh,	מִקְדַּשׁ מֶלֶךְ עִיר מְלוּכָה,
kumi tz'i mitoch ha-hafaychöh,	קוּמִי צְאִי מִתּוֹךְ הַהֲפֵכָה,
rav löch sheves b'aymek ha-böchö,	רַב לָךְ שֶׁבֶת בְּעֵמֶק הַבָּכָא,
v'hu yachmol öla-yich chemlöh.	וְהוּא יַחֲמוֹל עָלַיִךְ חֶמְלָה :

L'chöh dodi lik'ras kalöh,	לְכָה דוֹדִי לִקְרַאת כַּלָּה,
p'nay shabös n'kab'löh.	פְּנֵי שַׁבָּת נְקַבְּלָה :

Sanctuary of the King, royal city, arise, go forth from the ruins; too long have you dwelt in the vale of tears; He will show you abounding mercy. Come, my Beloved, to meet the Bride; let us welcome the Shabbat.

Hisna-ari may-öför kumi,	הִתְנַעֲרִי מֵעָפָר קוּמִי,
liv'shi big'day sif-artaych ami,	לִבְשִׁי בִּגְדֵי תִפְאַרְתֵּךְ עַמִּי,

al yad ben yi-shai bays ha-lachmi, עַל יַד בֶּן יִשַׁי בֵּית הַלַּחְמִי,

kör'vöh el nafshi g'ölöh. קָרְבָה אֶל נַפְשִׁי גְאָלָהּ :

L'chöh dodi lik'ras kalöh, לְכָה דוֹדִי לִקְרַאת כַּלָּה,

p'nay shabös n'kab'löh. פְּנֵי שַׁבָּת נְקַבְּלָה :

Shake the dust off yourself, arise, don your glorious garments — my people.
Through the son of Yishai of Beis Lechem, draw near to my soul and redeem it.
Come, my Beloved, to meet the Bride; let us welcome the Shabbat.

His-or'ri his-or'ri, הִתְעוֹרְרִי הִתְעוֹרְרִי,

ki vö oraych kumi ori, כִּי בָא אוֹרֵךְ קוּמִי אוֹרִי,

u-ri u-ri shir da-bayri, עוּרִי עוּרִי שִׁיר דַּבֵּרִי,

k'vod adonöy öla-yich niglöh. כְּבוֹד יְיָ עָלַיִךְ נִגְלָה :

L'chöh dodi lik'ras kalöh, לְכָה דוֹדִי לִקְרַאת כַּלָּה,

p'nay shabös n'kab'löh. פְּנֵי שַׁבָּת נְקַבְּלָה :

Arouse yourself, arouse yourself, for your light has come; arise, shine. Awake,
awake, utter a song; the glory of the Lord is revealed upon you. Come, my
Beloved, to meet the Bride; let us welcome the Shabbat.

Lo say-voshi v'lo siköl'mi, לֹא תֵבוֹשִׁי וְלֹא תִכָּלְמִי,

mah tish-tochachi umah te-hemi, מַה תִּשְׁתּוֹחֲחִי וּמַה תֶּהֱמִי,

böch ye-chesu ani-yay ami, בָּךְ יֶחֱסוּ עֲנִיֵּי עַמִּי,

v'niv-n'söh hö-ir al tilöh. וְנִבְנְתָה הָעִיר עַל תִּלָּהּ :

L'chöh dodi lik'ras kalöh, לְכָה דוֹדִי לִקְרַאת כַּלָּה,

p'nay shabös n'kab'löh. פְּנֵי שַׁבָּת נְקַבְּלָה :

64

The "Kabbalat Shabbat"

Do not be ashamed nor confounded; why are you downcast and why are you agitated? The afflicted of my people will find refuge in you; the city will be rebuilt on its former site. Come, my Beloved, to meet the Bride; let us welcome the Shabbat.

V'höyu lim'shisöh sho-sö-yich,	וְהָיוּ לִמְשִׁסָּה שֹׁאסָיִךְ,
v'röchaku köl m'val'ö-yich,	וְרָחֲקוּ כָּל מְבַלְּעָיִךְ,
yösis öla-yich elohö-yich,	יָשִׂישׂ עָלַיִךְ אֱלֹהָיִךְ,
kim'sos chösön al kalöh.	כִּמְשׂוֹשׂ חָתָן עַל כַּלָּה:
L'chöh dodi lik'ras kalöh,	לְכָה דוֹדִי לִקְרַאת כַּלָּה,
p'nay shabös n'kab'löh.	פְּנֵי שַׁבָּת נְקַבְּלָה:

Those who despoil you will be despoiled, and all who would destroy you will be far away. Your God will rejoice over you as a bridegroom rejoices over his bride. Come, my Beloved, to meet the Bride; let us welcome the Shabbat.

Yömin us'mol tifro-tzi,	יָמִין וּשְׂמֹאל תִּפְרוֹצִי,
v'es adonöy ta-ari-tzi,	וְאֶת יְיָ תַּעֲרִיצִי,
al yad ish ben par-tzi,	עַל יַד אִישׁ בֶּן פַּרְצִי,
v'nis-m'chöh v'nögiloh.	וְנִשְׂמְחָה וְנָגִילָה:
L'chöh dodi lik'ras kalöh,	לְכָה דוֹדִי לִקְרַאת כַּלָּה,
p'nay shabös n'kab'löh.	פְּנֵי שַׁבָּת נְקַבְּלָה:

To the right and to the left you shall spread out, and the Lord you shall extol. And we shall rejoice and exult, through the man who is a descendant of Peretz. Come, my Beloved, to meet the Bride; let us welcome the Shabbat.

Turn around, facing west, and say:

Bo-i v'shölom ateres ba'löh,   בּוֹאִי בְשָׁלוֹם עֲטֶרֶת בַּעְלָהּ,

gam b'rinöh (On Festivals substitue: גַּם בְּרִנָּה (ביו״ט: בְּשִׂמְחָה)

b'simchöh) uv'tzöhölöh, toch emunay   וּבְצָהֳלָה, תּוֹךְ אֱמוּנֵי

am s'gulöh, (Bow right) bo-i chalöh,   עַם סְגֻלָּה, בּוֹאִי כַלָּה,

(Bow left) bo-i chalöh, (Say silently a third   בּוֹאִי כַלָּה, (ויאמר בלחש

time:) bo-i chalöh   פעם שלישית בּוֹאִי כַלָּה

shabös mal-k'sö.   שַׁבָּת מַלְכְּתָא) :

Come in peace, O crown of her Husband, both with songs (On Festivals substitute: rejoicing) and gladness; among the faithful, the beloved people, (Bow right >) Come, O Bride, (Bow left <) come, O Bride, (Say silently a third time: come, O Bride; Shabbat Queen).

Turn back, facing east, bow forward, and say:

L'chöh dodi lik'ras kalöh,   לְכָה דוֹדִי לִקְרַאת כַּלָּה,

p'nay shabös n'kab'löh.   פְּנֵי שַׁבָּת נְקַבְּלָה :

Come, my beloved, to meet the Bride; let us welcome the Shabbat.

A Psalm, a Song...   מִזְמוֹר שִׁיר...

This Psalm celebrates the Shabbat day. A day on which we cease 'creating,' as God did on the seventh day of creation. This means not doing any of 39 kinds of creative physical activities and their offshoots, as listed in the Torah and explained in the Code of Jewish Law.

Mizmor shir l'yom ha-shabös. מִזְמוֹר שִׁיר לְיוֹם הַשַּׁבָּת:
Tov l'hodos la-donöy, ul'zamayr טוֹב לְהֹדוֹת לַיָי, וּלְזַמֵּר
l'shim'chö elyon. L'hagid ba-boker לְשִׁמְךָ עֶלְיוֹן: לְהַגִּיד בַּבֹּקֶר
chas-dechö, ve-emunös'chö ba-lay-los. חַסְדֶּךָ, וֶאֱמוּנָתְךָ בַּלֵּילוֹת:
Alay ösor va-alay növel, alay higö-yon עֲלֵי עָשׂוֹר וַעֲלֵי נָבֶל, עֲלֵי הִגָּיוֹן
b'chinor. Ki simach-tani adonöy בְּכִנּוֹר: כִּי שִׂמַּחְתַּנִי יְיָ
b'fö-ölechö, b'ma-asay yödechö בְּפָעֳלֶךָ, בְּמַעֲשֵׂי יָדֶיךָ
ara-nayn. Mah göd'lu ma-asechö אֲרַנֵּן: מַה גָּדְלוּ מַעֲשֶׂיךָ
adonöy, m'od öm'ku machsh'vosechö. יְיָ, מְאֹד עָמְקוּ מַחְשְׁבֹתֶיךָ:
Ish ba-ar lo yaydö, uch'sil lo yövin אִישׁ בַּעַר לֹא יֵדָע, וּכְסִיל לֹא יָבִין
es zos. Bifro-ach r'shö-im k'mo אֶת זֹאת: בִּפְרֹחַ רְשָׁעִים כְּמוֹ
aysev, va-yö-tzi-tzu köl po-alay öven, עֵשֶׂב, וַיָּצִיצוּ כָּל פֹּעֲלֵי אָוֶן,
l'hishöm'döm aday ad. V'atöh לְהִשָּׁמְדָם עֲדֵי עַד: וְאַתָּה
mörom l'olöm adonöy. Ki hinay מָרוֹם לְעֹלָם יְיָ: כִּי הִנֵּה
oy-vechö adonöy, ki hinay o-y'vechö אֹיְבֶיךָ יְיָ, כִּי הִנֵּה אֹיְבֶיךָ
yo-vaydu, yispör'du köl po-alay öven. יֹאבֵדוּ, יִתְפָּרְדוּ כָּל פֹּעֲלֵי אָוֶן:
Va-törem kir'aym karni, ba-losi וַתָּרֶם כִּרְאֵים קַרְנִי, בַּלֹּתִי
b'shemen ra-anön. Va-tabayt ayni בְּשֶׁמֶן רַעֲנָן: וַתַּבֵּט עֵינִי
b'shuröy, ba-kömim ölai m'rayim, בְּשׁוּרָי, בַּקָּמִים עָלַי מְרֵעִים,
tish-ma-nöh öznöy. Tzadik ka-tömör תִּשְׁמַעְנָה אָזְנָי: צַדִּיק כַּתָּמָר
yifröch, k'erez ba-l'vönon yisgeh. יִפְרָח, כְּאֶרֶז בַּלְּבָנוֹן יִשְׂגֶּה:
Sh'sulim b'vays adonöy, b'chatz'ros שְׁתוּלִים בְּבֵית יְיָ, בְּחַצְרוֹת
elohaynu yafrichu. Od y'nuvun אֱלֹהֵינוּ יַפְרִיחוּ: עוֹד יְנוּבוּן
b'sayvöh d'shaynim v'ra-ananim yihyu. בְּשֵׂיבָה, דְּשֵׁנִים וְרַעֲנַנִּים יִהְיוּ:

L'hagid ki yöshör adonöy,　　לְהַגִּיד כִּי יָשָׁר יְיָ,

tzuri v'lo avlösöh bo.　　צוּרִי וְלֹא עַוְלָתָה בּוֹ :

A Psalm, a song for the Shabbat day. It is good to praise the Lord, and to sing to Your Name, O Most High; to proclaim Your kindness in the morning, and Your faithfulness in the nights, with a ten-stringed instrument and lyre, to the melody of a harp. For You, Lord, have gladdened me with Your deeds; I sing for joy at the works of Your hand. How great are Your works, O Lord; how very profound Your thoughts! A brutish man cannot know, a fool cannot comprehend this: When the wicked thrive like grass, and all evildoers flourish — it is in order that they may be destroyed forever. But You, Lord, are exalted forever. Indeed, Your enemies, O Lord, indeed Your enemies shall perish; all evildoers shall be scattered. But You have increased my might like that of a wild ox; I am anointed with fresh oil. My eyes have seen [the downfall of] my watchful enemies; my ears have heard [the doom of] the wicked who rise against me. The righteous will flourish like a palm tree, grow tall like a cedar in Lebanon. Planted in the House of the Lord, they shall blossom in the courtyards of our God. They shall be fruitful even in old age; they shall be full of sap and freshness. That is to say that the Lord is just; He is my Strength, and there is no injustice in Him.

The Lord is King...　　...יְיָ מָלָךְ

This Psalm expresses the theme of God's sovereignty and strength.

Adonöy mölöch gay-us lö-vaysh,　　יְיָ מָלָךְ גֵּאוּת לָבֵשׁ,

lö-vaysh adonöy, oz his-azör, af tikon　　לָבֵשׁ יְיָ, עֹז הִתְאַזָּר, אַף תִּכּוֹן

tay-vayl bal timot. Nöchon kis-achö　　תֵּבֵל בַּל תִּמּוֹט : נָכוֹן כִּסְאֲךָ

may-öz, may-olöm ötöh. Nös'u מֵאָז, מֵעוֹלָם אָתָּה: נָשְׂאוּ
n'höros adonöy, nös'u n'höros נְהָרוֹת יְיָ, נָשְׂאוּ נְהָרוֹת
kolöm, yis'u n'höros döch-yöm. קוֹלָם, יִשְׂאוּ נְהָרוֹת דָּכְיָם:
Mikolos ma-yim rabim adirim מִקֹּלוֹת מַיִם רַבִּים אַדִּירִים
mishb'ray yöm, adir ba-mörom מִשְׁבְּרֵי יָם, אַדִּיר בַּמָּרוֹם
adonöy. Aydo-sechö ne-em'nu m'od, יְיָ: עֵדֹתֶיךָ נֶאֶמְנוּ מְאֹד,
l'vays'chö nö-avöh kodesh, לְבֵיתְךָ נַאֲוָה קֹדֶשׁ,
adonöy, l'orech yömim. יְיָ, לְאֹרֶךְ יָמִים:

The Lord is King; He has garbed Himself with grandeur; the Lord has robed Himself, He has girded Himself with strength; He has also established the world firmly that it shall not falter. Your throne stands firm from of old; You have existed forever. The rivers have raised, O Lord, the rivers have raised their voice; the rivers raise their raging waves. More than the sound of many waters, than the mighty breakers of the sea, is the Lord mighty on High. Your testimonies are most trustworthy; Your House will be resplendent in holiness, O Lord, forever.

Mourner's Kaddish קַדִּישׁ יָתוֹם

Recited standing, by mourners.

At specifically marked intervals during the prayers, when praying with a quorum of at least ten Jewish male adults, mourners recite this Kaddish. Kaddish means "holy." It was composed, like most of our prayers, by the Men of the Great Assembly. It is based on the wording of Ezekiel's prophecy in which *Kiddush Hashem*, the sanctification of God's Name, is

placed at the center of the national duty of Israel, upon which the deliverance of the Jewish nation was dependent. The word Amen, that the congregation responds, is like the word *Emunah*, which means belief, and by stating it we acknowledge that we believe what the reader has stated.

It is customary to bow the head while reciting specific words in the kaddish. These words are bracketed by the following symbol: " ° " In addition, one takes three steps back before "*Oseh Sholom*," and upon concluding the Kaddish, three steps forward. It is also customary to incline the head right, left, and straight ahead as indicated.

Yis-gadal v'yis-kadash °sh'may raböh°:	יִתְגַּדַּל וְיִתְקַדַּשׁ ∘שְׁמֵהּ רַבָּא∘:
(Cong: Ömayn)	אמן
B'öl'mö di v'rö chir'u-say	בְּעָלְמָא דִּי בְרָא כִרְעוּתֵהּ
v'yamlich mal'chusay, v'yatzmach	וְיַמְלִיךְ מַלְכוּתֵהּ, וְיַצְמַח
purkönay °vikörayv m'shi-chay°.	פּוּרְקָנֵהּ ∘וִיקָרֵב מְשִׁיחֵהּ∘:
(Cong: Ömayn)	אמן
B'cha-yay-chon uv'yomaychon.	בְּחַיֵּיכוֹן וּבְיוֹמֵיכוֹן
uv'chayay d'chöl bays yisrö-ayl,	וּבְחַיֵּי דְכָל בֵּית יִשְׂרָאֵל,
-agölö uviz'man köriv °v'im'ru ömayn°	בַּעֲגָלָא וּבִזְמַן קָרִיב ∘וְאִמְרוּ אָמֵן∘:
(Cong.: Ömayn. °Y'hay sh'may rabö m'vörach	אמן ∘יְהֵא שְׁמֵהּ רַבָּא מְבָרַךְ
l'ölam ul'öl'may öl'ma-yöh Yisböraych°).	לְעָלַם וּלְעָלְמֵי עָלְמַיָּא יִתְבָּרַךְ:
Yisböraych° °v'yishtabach, v'yispö-ayr,	יִתְבָּרַךְ∘ ∘וְיִשְׁתַּבַּח, וְיִתְפָּאַר,
v'yisromöm, v'yis-nasay, v'yis-hadör,	וְיִתְרוֹמָם, וְיִתְנַשֵּׂא, וְיִתְהַדָּר,
v'yis-aleh, v'yis-halöl°, °sh'may	וְיִתְעַלֶּה, וְיִתְהַלָּל∘, ∘שְׁמֵהּ
d'kud-shö b'rich hu°.	דְּקֻדְשָׁא בְּרִיךְ הוּא∘:
(Cong: Ömayn)	אמן

The "Kabbalat Shabbat"

L'aylö min köl bir'chösö v'shirösö, **לְעֵלָּא מִן כָּל בִּרְכָתָא וְשִׁירָתָא,**
tush-b'chösö v'ne-che-mösö, **תֻּשְׁבְּחָתָא וְנֶחֱמָתָא,**
da-amirön b'öl'mö, °v'im'ru ömayn°. **דַּאֲמִירָן בְּעָלְמָא, °וְאִמְרוּ אָמֵן°:**

(Cong: Ömayn) **אמן**

Y'hay sh'lömö rabö min sh'ma-yö, **יְהֵא שְׁלָמָא רַבָּא מִן שְׁמַיָּא**
v'cha-yim tovim ölaynu v'al köl **וְחַיִּים טוֹבִים עָלֵינוּ וְעַל כָּל**
yisrö-ayl °v'im'ru ömayn°. **יִשְׂרָאֵל °וְאִמְרוּ אָמֵן°:**

(Cong: Ömayn) **אמן**

>O-seh shölom **(Between Rosh Hashana** **>עֹשֶׂה שָׁלוֹם**
and Yom Kippur substitute: ha-shölom) **(בעשי״ת: הַשָּׁלוֹם)**
bim'romöv, ^hu <ya-aseh shölom **בִּמְרוֹמָיו, ^ הוּא <יַעֲשֶׂה**
ölaynu ^v'al köl yisrö-ayl, **שָׁלוֹם עָלֵינוּ ^וְעַל כָּל יִשְׂרָאֵל,**
°v'im'ru ömayn°. **(Cong: Ömayn)** **°וְאִמְרוּ אָמֵן°: אמן**

*Exalted and hallowed be His great Name (**Cong: Amen.**) throughout the world which He has created according to His will. May He establish His kingship, bring forth His redemption and hasten the coming of His Moshiach (**Cong: Amen.**) in your lifetime and in your days and in the lifetime of the entire House of Israel, speedily and soon, and say, Amen. (**Cong: Amen.** May His great Name be blessed forever and to all eternity. Blessed.) May His great Name be blessed forever and to all eternity. Blessed and praised, glorified, exalted and extolled, honored, adored and lauded be the Name of the Holy One, blessed be He, (**Cong: Amen.**) beyond all the blessings, hymns, praises and consolations that are uttered in the world; and say, Amen. (**Cong: Amen.**) May there be abundant peace from heaven, and a good life for us and for all Israel; and say, Amen. (**Cong: Amen.**) He who makes peace (**Between Rosh Hashana and Yom Kippur substitute: the peace**) in His heavens, may He make peace for us and for all Israel; and say, Amen. (**Cong: Amen.**)*

Just As They...   ...כְּגַוְנָא דְאִנּוּן

These are profoundly mystical kabbalistic passages, difficult to explain adequately here, especially since they are only a small section of a larger context. Suffice it to say that it describes the Divine attributes as they evolve with the approach of the Shabbat.

K'gavnö d'inun mis-yachadin l'aylö	כְּגַוְנָא דְאִנּוּן מִתְיַחֲדִין לְעֵלָּא
b'echöd uf höchi ihi isya-chadas	בְּאֶחָד אוּף הָכִי אִיהִי אִתְיַחֲדַת
l'satö b'rözö d'echöd l'mehevay	לְתַתָּא בְּרָזָא דְאֶחָד לְמֶהֱוֵי
im'hon l'aylö chöd lökövayl chöd,	עִמְּהוֹן לְעֵלָּא חַד לָקֳבֵל חָד,
kud-shö b'rich hu echöd l'aylö lö	קוּדְשָׁא בְּרִיךְ הוּא אֶחָד לְעֵלָּא לָא
y'siv al kursa-yö diköray ad	יְתִיב עַל כּוּרְסַיָּא דִיקָרֵיהּ עַד
d'is-avidas ihi b'rözö d'echöd	דְּאִתְעֲבִידַת אִיהִי בְּרָזָא דְאֶחָד
k'gavnö dilay l'mehevay echöd	כְּגַוְנָא דִילֵיהּ לְמֶהֱוֵי אֶחָד
b'echöd. V'hö ukimnö rözö	בְּאֶחָד. וְהָא אוּקִימְנָא רָזָא
da-adonöy echöd ush'mö echöd.	דַיְיָ אֶחָד וּשְׁמוֹ אֶחָד.

Just as they [the six sefirot: chesed (kindness) yesod (foundation)] unite above into oneness, so she [malchut (kingship)] unites below into the mystery of oneness, so as to be with them above — unity paralleling unity. The Holy One, blessed be He, who is One above, does not take His seat upon His Throne of Glory until she enters into the mystery of oneness, similar to His, to be oneness corresponding to Oneness. This, as we have stated, is the esoteric meaning of the words: "The Lord is One, and His Name is One."

Rözö d'shabös ihi shabös
d'is-öchödas b'rözö d'echöd
l'mishray alöh rözö d'echöd. Tz'losö
d'ma-alay shabatö d'hö is-öchödas
kursa-yö yakirö kadishö b'rözö
d'echöd, v'ista-könas l'mishray alöh
malkö kadishö ilö-ö. Kad a-yil
shabatö ihi is-yöchödas v'isp'röshas
mi-sitrö öchörö. V'chöl dinin
mis-ab'rin minöh v'ihi ish-t'öras
b'yichudö din'hiru kadishö v'is-at'ras
b'chamö itrin l'gabay malkö kadishö.
V'chöl shultönay rugzin umöray
d'dinö kul'hu arkin v'is-aböru minöh.
V'lays shultönö öchörö b'chul'hu
öl'min, v'anpöhö n'hirin bin'hiru
ilö-ö v'is-at'ras l'satö b'amö
kadishö. V'chul'hu mis-at'rin
b'nishmosin chadatin. K'dayn
shayrusö ditz'losö l'vör'chö
löh b'chedvöh bin'hiru d'anpin.

רָזָא דְשַׁבָּת אִיהִי שַׁבָּת
דְּאִתְאֲחָדַת בְּרָזָא דְּאֶחָד
לְמִשְׁרֵי עֲלָהּ רָזָא דְּאֶחָד. צְלוֹתָא
דְמַעֲלֵי שַׁבַּתָּא דְּהָא אִתְאַחֲדַת
כּוּרְסַיָּא יַקִּירָא קַדִּישָׁא בְּרָזָא
דְּאֶחָד, וְאִתְתַּקְּנַת לְמִשְׁרֵי עֲלָהּ
מַלְכָּא קַדִּישָׁא עִלָּאָה. כַּד עָיֵל
שַׁבַּתָּא אִיהִי אִתְיָחֲדַת וְאִתְפְּרָשַׁת
מִסִּטְרָא אָחֳרָא. וְכָל דִּינִין
מִתְעַבְּרִין מִנָּהּ וְאִיהִי אִשְׁתְּאָרַת
בְּיִחוּדָא דִּנְהִירוּ קַדִּישָׁא וְאִתְעַטְּרַת
בְּכַמָּה עִטְרִין לְגַבֵּי מַלְכָּא קַדִּישָׁא.
וְכָל שׁוּלְטָנֵי רוּגְזִין וּמָארֵי
דְּדִינָא כֻּלְּהוּ עַרְקִין וְאִתְעֲבָרוּ מִנָּהּ.
וְלֵית שׁוּלְטָנָא אָחֳרָא בְּכֻלְּהוּ
עָלְמִין, וְאַנְפָּהָא נְהִירִין בִּנְהִירוּ
עִלָּאָה וְאִתְעַטְּרַת לְתַתָּא בְּעַמָּא
קַדִּישָׁא. וְכֻלְּהוּ מִתְעַטְּרִין
בְּנִשְׁמָתִין חֲדַתִּין. כְּדֵין
שֵׁירוּתָא דִּצְלוֹתָא לְבָרְכָא
לָהּ בְּחֶדְוָה בִּנְהִירוּ דְּאַנְפִּין:

*The mystery of Shabbat: She [the Sefira of malchut] is on Shabbat united
within the mystery of Oneness so that the [supernal] mystery of Oneness may
rest upon her. [This takes place during] the Maariv Prayer of Shabbat eve, for*

then the holy Throne of Glory merges into the mystery of Oneness, and is ready for the holy transcendent King to rest upon it. As Shabbat arrives, she merges into Oneness, and is separated from the "other side," and all strict judgments are severed from her. And she remains in unity with the holy light, and crowns herself with many crowns for the holy King. Then all powers of wrath and all adversaries flee from her and vanish, and no other power reigns in any of the worlds. Her countenance is irradiated with a supernal light, and she crowns herself here below with the holy people, all of whom are crowned with new souls. Then the commencement of the prayer is to bless her with joy and radiant countenance.

Continue on page 76.

And Say...

וְלוֹמַר בָּרְכוּ...

Recited when praying alone or without a Minyan

This seleton is meant to stand in place of the *Bor'chu* call to prayer, which can only be recited with a Minyan.

וְלוֹמַר בָּרְכוּ אֶת יְיָ
הַמְבוֹרָךְ, אֶת דַּיְקָא דָא שַׁבָּת
דְּמַעֲלֵי שַׁבַּתָּא : בָּרוּךְ יְיָ
הַמְבֹרָךְ דָּא אַפִּיקוּ דְבִרְכָאן
מִמְּקוֹרָא דְחַיֵּי וַאֲתַר דְּנָפִיק
מִנֵּיהּ כָּל שַׁקְיוּ לְאַשְׁקָאָה לְכֹלָּא.
וּבְגִין דְּאִיהוּ מְקוֹרָא בְּרָזָא דְאָת
קַיָּמָא קָרִינָן לֵיהּ הַמְבָרַךְ אִיהוּ
מַבּוּעָא דְבֵירָא וְכֵיוָן דִּמְטָאן
הָתָם הָא כֻּלְּהוּ לְעוֹלָם וָעֶד.
וְדָא אִיהוּ בָּרוּךְ יְיָ
הַמְבֹרָךְ לְעוֹלָם וָעֶד :

V'lomar bö-r'chu es adonöy
ha-m'voröch, es daikö dö shabös
d'ma-alay sha-batö. Böruch adonöy
ha-m'voröch dö apiku d'vir-chö-ön
mim'körö d'cha-yay va-asar d'nöfik
minay köl shak-yu l'ashkö-ö l'cholö.
Uv'gin d'ihu m'körö b'rözö d'ös
ka-yömö körinön lay ha-m'voröch ihu
mabu-ö d'vayrö v'chayvön dim'tö-ön
hösöm hö chul'hu l'olöm vö-ed.
V'dö ihu Böruch adonöy
ha-m'voröch l'olöm vö-ed.

And say: "Bless the Lord who is blessed". The word "the" refers to Shabbat eve. "Blessed be the Lord who is blessed" is that which elicits the blessings from the source of life and the place from whence issue all streams to irrigate all things. And because it is the source, the mystery of the "sign," it is called "the blessed." It is the stream of the wellspring. And since they [the blessings] reach there, they all [flow] "for all eternity." And this is [the meaning of]: "Blessed be the Lord who is blessed for all eternity."

The Shabbat and Festival Evening Services

The evening service consists of: the Shema, with two blessings before and two after it, the Amidah, special Shabbat portions, and concluding prayers.

The leader recites Half Kaddish followed by *Bor'chu* (Bless...). *Bor'chu* is a summons, or call, by the leader to join him in praising God. It is explained in *Kabbalah* that all mitzvot require proper preparation; we do not want to perform the sacred mitzvot without proper mental preparation. We take time to pause and think of the great significance of the mitzvah we are about to perform. This same benediction is said once again at the end of the Shabbat evening prayer, for those who have tarried in coming to the synagogue (they were occupied preparing for the Shabbat) and have not heard its first recital.

A Song of Ascents ...   ... שִׁיר הַמַּעֲלוֹת

Weekday Festival services begin here

(When the Festival occures on Shabbat, the services begin earlier with *Mizmor L'Dovid*, 'A Psalm by David' on page 58.)

Shir ha-ma-alos, hinay bö-r'chu	שִׁיר הַמַּעֲלוֹת, הִנֵּה בָּרְכוּ
es adonöy köl av'day adonöy	אֶת יְיָ כָּל עַבְדֵי יְיָ
hö-öm'dim b'vays adonöy ba-laylos.	הָעֹמְדִים בְּבֵית יְיָ בַּלֵּילוֹת:
S'u y'daychem kodesh, uvö-r'chu	שְׂאוּ יְדֵכֶם קֹדֶשׁ, וּבָרְכוּ

76

es adonöy. Y'vö-rech'chö adonöy אֶת יְיָ : יְבָרֶכְךָ יְיָ

mitziyon, osay shöma-yim vö-öretz. מִצִיּוֹן, עֹשֵׂה שָׁמַיִם וָאָרֶץ :

Yomöm y'tza-veh adonöy chasdo יוֹמָם יְצַוֶּה יְיָ חַסְדּוֹ

uvalai-löh shiroh imi t'filöh l'ayl וּבַלַּיְלָה שִׁירֹה עִמִּי תְּפִלָּה לְאֵל

cha-yöy.Us'shu-as tzadikim חַיָּי : וּתְשׁוּעַת צַדִּיקִים

may-donöy mö-uzöm b'ays tzöröh. מֵיְיָ מָעוּזָּם בְּעֵת צָרָה :

Va-ya-z'raym adonöy va-y'fal'taym, וַיַּעְזְרֵם יְיָ וַיְפַלְטֵם,

y'fal'taym may-r'shö-im v'yoshi-aym, יְפַלְטֵם מֵרְשָׁעִים וְיוֹשִׁיעֵם,

ki chösu vo. Adonöy tz'vö-os כִּי חָסוּ בוֹ : יְיָ צְבָאוֹת

imönu, misgöv lönu elohay עִמָּנוּ מִשְׂגָּב לָנוּ אֱלֹהֵי

ya-akov selöh. **Say three times.** יַעֲקֹב סֶלָה ג"פ :

Adonöy tzvö-os ash-ray ödöm יְיָ צְבָאוֹת אַשְׁרֵי אָדָם

botay-ach böch. **Say three times.** בֹּטֵחַ בָּךְ ג"פ :

Adonöy hoshi-öh, יְיָ הוֹשִׁיעָה,

ha-melech ya-anaynu v'yom הַמֶּלֶךְ יַעֲנֵנוּ בְיוֹם

kör'aynu. **Say three times.** קָרְאֵנוּ ג"פ :

*A Song of Ascents. Bless the Lord, all servants of the Lord who stand in the house of the Lord at night. Raise your hands in holiness and bless the Lord. May the Lord, Maker of heaven and earth, bless you from Zion. By day the Lord ordains His kindness, and at night His song is with me, a prayer to the God of my life. The deliverance of the righteous is from the Lords; He is their strength in time of distress. The Lord helps them and delivers them; He delivers them from the wicked and saves them, because they have put their trust in Him. **Say three times:** The Lord of hosts is with us; the God of Jacob is our stronghold forever. **Say three times:** Lord of hosts, happy is the man who trusts in You. **Say three times:** Lord, deliver us; may the King answer us on the day we call.*

Leader's Half-Kaddish

חֲצִי קַדִּישׁ

The leader recites the Half-Kaddish below, followed by *Bor'chu* (Bless...).

Yis-gadal v'yis-kadash °sh'may raböh°:	יִתְגַּדַּל וְיִתְקַדַּשׁ ° שְׁמֵהּ רַבָּא ° :
(Cong: Ömayn)	אמן
B'öl'mö di v'rö chir'u-say	בְּעָלְמָא דִּי בְרָא כִרְעוּתֵהּ
v'yamlich mal'chusay, v'yatzmach	וְיַמְלִיךְ מַלְכוּתֵהּ, וְיַצְמַח
purkönay °viköryv m'shi-chay°:	פּוּרְקָנֵהּ ° וִיקָרֵב מְשִׁיחֵהּ ° :
(Cong: Ömayn)	אמן
B'cha-yay-chon uv'yomaychon.	בְּחַיֵּיכוֹן וּבְיוֹמֵיכוֹן
uv'chayay d'chöl bays yisrö-ayl,	וּבְחַיֵּי דְכָל בֵּית יִשְׂרָאֵל,
-agölö uviz'man köriv °v'im'ru ömayn°	בַּעֲגָלָא וּבִזְמַן קָרִיב ° וְאִמְרוּ אָמֵן ° :
(Cong.: Ömayn. °Y'hay sh'may rabö m'vörach	אמן ° יְהֵא שְׁמֵהּ רַבָּא מְבָרַךְ
l'ölam ul'öl'may öl'ma-yöh Yisböraych°).	לְעָלַם וּלְעָלְמֵי עָלְמַיָּא יִתְבָּרַךְ ° :
Yisböraych° °v'yishtabach, v'yispö-ayr,	יִתְבָּרַךְ ° ° וְיִשְׁתַּבַּח, וְיִתְפָּאַר,
v'yisromöm, v'yis-nasay, v'yis-hadör,	וְיִתְרוֹמָם, וְיִתְנַשֵּׂא, וְיִתְהַדָּר,
v'yis-aleh, v'yis-halöl°, °sh'may	וְיִתְעַלֶּה, וְיִתְהַלָּל ° , ° שְׁמֵהּ
d'kud-shö b'rich hu°.	דְּקֻדְשָׁא בְּרִיךְ הוּא ° :
(Cong: Ömayn)	אמן
L'aylö min köl bir'chöso v'shiröso,	לְעֵלָּא מִן כָּל בִּרְכָתָא וְשִׁירָתָא,
tush-b'chöso v'ne-che-mösö,	תֻּשְׁבְּחָתָא וְנֶחֱמָתָא,
da-amirön b'öl'mö, °v'im'ru ömayn°.	דַּאֲמִירָן בְּעָלְמָא, ° וְאִמְרוּ אָמֵן ° :
(Cong: Ömayn)	אמן

78

Exalted and hallowed be His great Name (Cong: Amen.) *throughout the world which He has created according to His will. May He establish His kingship, bring forth His redemption and hasten the coming of His Moshiach* (Cong: Amen.) *In your lifetime and in your days and in the lifetime of the entire House of Israel, speedily and soon, and say, Amen.* (Cong: Amen. May His great Name be blessed forever and to all eternity. Blessed.) *May His great Name be blessed forever and to all eternity. Blessed and praised, glorified, exalted and extolled, honored, adored and lauded be the Name of the Holy One, blessed be He,* (Cong: Amen.) *Beyond all the blessings, hymns, praises and consolations that are uttered in the world; and say, Amen.*

Bor'chu is recited standing. When saying the words, we bow in reverence to God.

Leader:	חזן:
Bö-r'chu es adonöy ha-m'voröch.	בָּרְכוּ אֶת יְיָ הַמְבֹרָךְ:
Congregation and leader:	קהל וחזן:
Böruch adonöy ha-m'voröch	בָּרוּךְ יְיָ הַמְבֹרָךְ
l'olöm vö-ed.	לְעוֹלָם וָעֶד:

Leader: *Bless the Lord who is blessed.* Congregation and Leader: *Blessed be the Lord who is blessed for all eternity.*

Blessed Are You...   בָּרוּךְ אַתָּה...

Recited Seated

This is the first blessing before the *Shema*. With this blessing we acknowledge the awesome change from day to night. The opening verse

refers to the first evening which God created, as it is written in Genesis, "And it was evening, and it was morning, one day." What may seem as a 'natural' and 'ordinary' change from day to night and from night to day, from summer to winter, and from winter to summer, and so on, is really a wonderful act of Creation by God, not something to be taken for granted.

בָּרוּךְ אַתָּה יְיָ אֱלֹהֵינוּ מֶלֶךְ הָעוֹלָם, אֲשֶׁר בִּדְבָרוֹ מַעֲרִיב עֲרָבִים, בְּחָכְמָה פּוֹתֵחַ שְׁעָרִים, וּבִתְבוּנָה מְשַׁנֶּה עִתִּים, וּמַחֲלִיף אֶת הַזְּמַנִּים, וּמְסַדֵּר אֶת הַכּוֹכָבִים, בְּמִשְׁמְרוֹתֵיהֶם בָּרָקִיעַ, כִּרְצוֹנוֹ. בּוֹרֵא יוֹם וָלַיְלָה, גּוֹלֵל אוֹר מִפְּנֵי חֹשֶׁךְ, וְחֹשֶׁךְ מִפְּנֵי אוֹר, וּמַעֲבִיר יוֹם וּמֵבִיא לָיְלָה, וּמַבְדִּיל בֵּין יוֹם וּבֵין לָיְלָה, יְיָ צְבָאוֹת שְׁמוֹ. בָּרוּךְ אַתָּה יְיָ, הַמַּעֲרִיב עֲרָבִים:

Böruch atöh adonöy elohaynu melech hö-olöm, asher bid'vöro ma-ariv arövim, b'chöchmöh posay-ach sh'örim, uvis-vunöh m'sha-neh itim, umacha-lif es ha-z'manim, um'sader es ha-kochövim, b'mish-m'rosay-hem böröki-ah, kir'tzono. Boray yom völöy-löh, golayl or mip'nay cho-shech, v'cho-shech mip'nay or, uma-avir yom umay-vi löy-löh, umavdil bayn yom uvayn löy-löh, adonöy tzvö-os sh'mo. Böruch atöh adonöy, ha-ma-ariv arövim.

Blessed are You, Lord our God, King of the universe, who by His word causes the evenings to become dark. With wisdom He opens the [heavenly] gates; with understanding He changes the periods [of the day], varies the times, and arranges the stars in their positions in the sky according to His will. He creates day and night; He rolls away light before darkness and darkness before light; He causes the

day to pass and brings on the night, and separates between day and night; the Lord of hosts is His Name. Blessed are You Lord, who causes the evenings to become dark.

With Everlasting Love...

אַהֲבַת עוֹלָם ...

This blessing is a fitting introduction to the Shema. It speaks of God's love to us, His people, and reminds us that the Torah and Mitzvot are not merely additions to our life, but our very life and only cause for existence.

אַהֲבַת עוֹלָם בֵּית יִשְׂרָאֵל עַמְּךָ
אָהָבְתָּ, תּוֹרָה וּמִצְוֹת, חֻקִּים
וּמִשְׁפָּטִים אוֹתָנוּ לִמַּדְתָּ:
עַל כֵּן יְיָ אֱלֹהֵינוּ,
בְּשָׁכְבֵנוּ וּבְקוּמֵנוּ
נָשִׂיחַ בְּחֻקֶּיךָ, וְנִשְׂמַח
בְּדִבְרֵי תוֹרָתֶךָ וּבְמִצְוֹתֶיךָ
לְעוֹלָם וָעֶד: כִּי הֵם חַיֵּינוּ
וְאֹרֶךְ יָמֵינוּ, וּבָהֶם נֶהְגֶּה
יוֹמָם וָלַיְלָה, וְאַהֲבָתְךָ לֹא
תָסוּר מִמֶּנּוּ לְעוֹלָמִים: בָּרוּךְ
אַתָּה יְיָ, אוֹהֵב עַמּוֹ יִשְׂרָאֵל:

Ahavas olöm bays yisrö-ayl am'chö
öhövtö, toröh umitzvos, chukim
umishpötim osönu limad-tö.
Al kayn adonöy elohaynu,
b'shöch'vaynu uv'kumaynu
nösi-ach b'chukechö, v'nismach
b'div'ray sorös'chö uv'mitzvo-sechö
l'olöm vö-ed. Ki haym cha-yaynu
v'orech yömaynu, uvöhem neh-geh
yomöm völöy-lö, v'ahavös'chö lo
sösur mi-menu l'olömim. Boruch
atöh adonöy, ohayv amo yisrö-ayl.

With everlasting love have You loved the House of Israel Your people. You have taught us Torah and mitzvot, decrees and laws. Therefore, Lord our God, when we lie down and when we rise, we will speak of Your statutes and rejoice in the words of Your Torah and in Your mitzvot forever. For they are our life and the length of

our days, and we will meditate on them day and night. May Your love never depart from us. Blessed are You Lord, who loves His people Israel.

Hear, O Israel...   ...שְׁמַע יִשְׂרָאֵל

The Shema is the essence of our faith. It consists of three paragraphs taken from the Bible. The first paragraph begins with the proclamation: "The Lord is One." It goes on to tell us that we must love God and dedicate our lives to the carrying out of his will. We can keep this faith alive only if we bring up our children in this belief. This section also contains the two mitzvot of Tefillin and Mezuzah, which remind us that we are Jews.

The second chapter contains a promise that if we fulfill and observe God's commands we shall be a happy people in our land. If not, we will suffer exile and hardships in strange lands, so that by suffering and trouble we will learn the ways of God and return to Him. We are again reminded to teach our children our true faith, and the Tefillin and Mezuzah are again mentioned, because they are the symbols of practical observance of God's commands.

The third chapter contains the commandment of Tzitzit, the distinctive Jewish garment which is a constant reminder of all the precepts of the Torah. We are also reminded that God brought us out of Egypt and made us His people, and that we accepted Him as our God.

It is customary to cover the eyes with the right hand while reciting the first verse of the *Shema*, to promote deep concentration.

Sh'ma yisrö-ayl, adonöy   שְׁמַע יִשְׂרָאֵל, יְיָ
elohaynu, adonöy echöd.   אֱלֹהֵינוּ, יְיָ אֶחָד:

Hear, O Israel, the Lord is our God, the Lord is One.

Remove the hand from the eyes, and say the following in an undertone:

Böruch shaym k'vod   בָּרוּךְ שֵׁם כְּבוֹד

mal'chuso l'olöm vö-ed.   מַלְכוּתוֹ לְעוֹלָם וָעֶד :

Blessed be the name of the glory of His kingdom forever and ever.

Continue in a regular tone below:

V'öhavtö ays adonöy elohechö,   וְאָהַבְתָּ אֵת יְיָ אֱלֹהֶיךָ,

b'chöl l'vöv'chö, uv'chöl   בְּכָל לְבָבְךָ, וּבְכָל

naf-sh'chö, uv'chöl m'odechö.   נַפְשְׁךָ, וּבְכָל מְאֹדֶךָ :

V'hö-yu ha-d'vörim hö-ay-leh asher   וְהָיוּ הַדְּבָרִים הָאֵלֶּה אֲשֶׁר

önochi m'tzav'chö ha-yom, al   אָנֹכִי מְצַוְּךָ הַיּוֹם, עַל

l'vö-vechö. V'shinan-töm l'vö-nechö   לְבָבֶךָ : וְשִׁנַּנְתָּם לְבָנֶיךָ

v'dibartö böm, b'shiv-t'chö   וְדִבַּרְתָּ בָּם, בְּשִׁבְתְּךָ

b'vaysechö, uv'lech-t'chö vaderech,   בְּבֵיתֶךָ, וּבְלֶכְתְּךָ בַדֶּרֶךְ,

uv'shöch-b'chö, uv'kumechö.   וּבְשָׁכְבְּךָ, וּבְקוּמֶךָ :

Uk'shartöm l'os al yödechö, v'hö-yu   וּקְשַׁרְתָּם לְאוֹת עַל יָדֶךָ, וְהָיוּ

l'totöfos bayn aynechö. Uch'savtöm   לְטֹטָפֹת בֵּין עֵינֶיךָ : וּכְתַבְתָּם

al m'zuzos bay-sechö, uvish'örechö.   עַל מְזֻזוֹת בֵּיתֶךָ, וּבִשְׁעָרֶיךָ :

You shall love the Lord your God with all your heart, with all your soul, and with all your might. And these words which I command you today shall be upon your heart. You shall teach them thoroughly to your children, and you shall speak of them when you sit in your house and when you walk on the road, when you lie down and when you rise. You shall bind them as a sign upon your hand, and they shall be for a reminder between your eyes. And you shall write them upon the doorposts of your house and upon your gates.

V'hö-yöh im shömo-a tish-m'u
el mitzvo-sai asher önochi m'tza-veh
es'chem ha-yom, l'ahavöh es adonöy
elohaychem ul'öv'do, b'chöl
l'vav'chem uv'chöl naf-sh'chem.
V'nösati m'tar artz'chem b'ito yo-reh
umalkosh, v'ösaftö d'gönechö
v'sirosh'chö v'yitz-hörechö. V'nösati
aysev b'söd'chö liv'hemtechö,
v'öchaltö v'sövö-tö. Hishöm'ru
löchem pen yifteh l'vav'chem,
v'sartem va-avad-tem elohim
achayrim v'hish-tachavisem löhem.
V'chöröh af adonöy böchem v'ötzar
es ha-shöma-yim v'lo yih-yeh mötör
v'hö-adömöh lo sitayn es y'vulöh,
va-avad-tem m'hayröh may-al
hö-öretz ha-tovöh asher adonöy
nosayn löchem. V'samtem es d'vörai
ayleh al l'vav'chem v'al naf-sh'chem
uk'shartem osöm l'os al yed'chem
v'hö-yu l'totöfos bayn aynaychem.
V'limad-tem osöm es b'naychem
l'dabayr böm, b'shiv-t'chö b'vaysechö

וְהָיָה אִם שָׁמֹעַ תִּשְׁמְעוּ
אֶל מִצְוֹתַי אֲשֶׁר אָנֹכִי מְצַוֶּה
אֶתְכֶם הַיּוֹם, לְאַהֲבָה אֶת יְיָ
אֱלֹהֵיכֶם וּלְעָבְדוֹ, בְּכָל
לְבַבְכֶם וּבְכָל נַפְשְׁכֶם :
וְנָתַתִּי מְטַר אַרְצְכֶם בְּעִתּוֹ יוֹרֶה
וּמַלְקוֹשׁ, וְאָסַפְתָּ דְגָנֶךָ
וְתִירשְׁךָ וְיִצְהָרֶךָ : וְנָתַתִּי
עֵשֶׂב בְּשָׂדְךָ לִבְהֶמְתֶּךָ,
וְאָכַלְתָּ וְשָׂבָעְתָּ : הִשָּׁמְרוּ
לָכֶם פֶּן יִפְתֶּה לְבַבְכֶם,
וְסַרְתֶּם וַעֲבַדְתֶּם אֱלֹהִים
אֲחֵרִים וְהִשְׁתַּחֲוִיתֶם לָהֶם :
וְחָרָה אַף יְיָ בָּכֶם וְעָצַר
אֶת הַשָּׁמַיִם וְלֹא יִהְיֶה מָטָר
וְהָאֲדָמָה לֹא תִתֵּן אֶת יְבוּלָהּ
וַאֲבַדְתֶּם מְהֵרָה מֵעַל
הָאָרֶץ הַטֹּבָה אֲשֶׁר יְיָ
נֹתֵן לָכֶם : וְשַׂמְתֶּם אֶת דְּבָרַי
אֵלֶּה עַל לְבַבְכֶם וְעַל נַפְשְׁכֶם
וּקְשַׁרְתֶּם אֹתָם לְאוֹת עַל יֶדְכֶם
וְהָיוּ לְטוֹטָפֹת בֵּין עֵינֵיכֶם :
וְלִמַּדְתֶּם אֹתָם אֶת בְּנֵיכֶם
לְדַבֵּר בָּם, בְּשִׁבְתְּךָ בְּבֵיתֶךָ

uv'lech-t'chö vaderech	וּבְלֶכְתְּךָ בַדֶּרֶךְ
uv'shöch-b'chö uv'kumechö.	וּבְשָׁכְבְּךָ וּבְקוּמֶךָ :
Uch'savtöm al m'zuzos baysechö	וּכְתַבְתָּם עַל מְזוּזוֹת בֵּיתֶךָ
uvish'örechö. L'ma-an yirbu	וּבִשְׁעָרֶיךָ : לְמַעַן יִרְבּוּ
y'maychem vimay v'naychem al	יְמֵיכֶם וִימֵי בְנֵיכֶם עַל
hö-adömöh asher nishba adonöy	הָאֲדָמָה אֲשֶׁר נִשְׁבַּע יְיָ
la-avosaychem lösays löhem,	לַאֲבֹתֵיכֶם לָתֵת לָהֶם,
kimay ha-shöma-yim al hö-öretz.	כִּימֵי הַשָּׁמַיִם עַל הָאָרֶץ :

And it will be, if you will diligently obey My commandments which I enjoin upon you this day, to love the Lord your God and to serve Him with all your heart and with all your soul, I will give rain for your land at the proper time, the early rain and the late rain, and you will gather in your grain, your wine and your oil. And I will give grass in your fields for your cattle, and you will eat and be sated. Take care lest your heart be lured away, and you turn astray and worship alien gods and bow down to them. For then the Lord's wrath will flare up against you, and He will close the heavens so that there will be no rain and the earth will not yield its produce, and you will swiftly perish from the good land which the Lord gives you. Therefore, place these words of Mine upon your heart and upon your soul, and bind them for a sign on your hand, and they shall be for a reminder between your eyes. You shall teach them to your children, to speak of them when you sit in your house and when you walk on the road, when you lie down and when you rise. And you shall inscribe them on the doorposts of your house and on your gates — so that your days and the days of your children may be prolonged on the land which the Lord swore to your fathers to give to them for as long as the heavens are above the earth.

85

Va-yomer adonöy el mosheh laymor.
Dabayr el b'nay yisrö-ayl v'ömartö
alay-hem v'ösu löhem tzitzis al
kan'fay vig'dayhem l'dorosöm,
v'nös'nu al tzitzis ha-könöf,
p'sil t'chayles. V'hö-yöh löchem
l'tzitzis, ur'isem oso uz'chartem
es köl mitzvos adonöy va-asisem
osöm, v'lo sösuru acha-ray
l'vav'chem v'acharay aynay-chem
asher atem zonim acha-rayhem.
L'ma-an tiz-k'ru va-asisem es
köl mitzvo-söy, vih-yisem k'doshim
laylo-haychem. Ani adonöy
elo-haychem asher ho-tzaysi es'chem
may-eretz mitzra-yim lih-yos löchem
laylohim, ani adonöy elo-haychem.
Emes.

וַיֹּאמֶר יְיָ אֶל מֹשֶׁה לֵּאמֹר:
דַּבֵּר אֶל בְּנֵי יִשְׂרָאֵל וְאָמַרְתָּ
אֲלֵהֶם וְעָשׂוּ לָהֶם צִיצִת עַל
כַּנְפֵי בִגְדֵיהֶם לְדֹרֹתָם,
וְנָתְנוּ עַל צִיצִת הַכָּנָף,
פְּתִיל תְּכֵלֶת: וְהָיָה לָכֶם
לְצִיצִת, וּרְאִיתֶם אֹתוֹ וּזְכַרְתֶּם
אֶת כָּל מִצְוֹת יְיָ וַעֲשִׂיתֶם
אֹתָם, וְלֹא תָתוּרוּ אַחֲרֵי
לְבַבְכֶם וְאַחֲרֵי עֵינֵיכֶם
אֲשֶׁר אַתֶּם זֹנִים אַחֲרֵיהֶם:
לְמַעַן תִּזְכְּרוּ וַעֲשִׂיתֶם אֶת
כָּל מִצְוֹתָי, וִהְיִיתֶם קְדֹשִׁים
לֵאלֹהֵיכֶם: אֲנִי יְיָ
אֱלֹהֵיכֶם אֲשֶׁר הוֹצֵאתִי אֶתְכֶם
מֵאֶרֶץ מִצְרַיִם לִהְיוֹת לָכֶם
לֵאלֹהִים, אֲנִי יְיָ אֱלֹהֵיכֶם:
אֱמֶת.

The Lord spoke to Moses, saying: Speak to the children of Israel and tell them to make for themselves fringes on the corners of their garments throughout their generations, and to attach a thread of blue on the fringe of each corner. They shall be to you as tzitzit, and you shall look upon them and remember all the commandments of the Lord and fulfill them, and you will not follow after your heart and after your eyes by which you go astray — so that you may remember and fulfill all My commandments and be holy to your God. I am the

Lord your God who brought you out of the land of Egypt to be your God; I, the Lord, am your God. Truth...

Truth and Belief...

אֱמֶת וֶאֱמוּנָה...

This section refers to the Shema we just read. It reinforces our connection and belief in God and recounts the numerous miracles He has wrought for the Jewish people which enabled us to be here today.

וֶאֱמוּנָה כָּל זֹאת, וְקַיָּם
עָלֵינוּ, כִּי הוּא יְיָ אֱלֹהֵינוּ
וְאֵין זוּלָתוֹ, וַאֲנַחְנוּ יִשְׂרָאֵל
עַמּוֹ, הַפּוֹדֵנוּ מִיַּד מְלָכִים,
מַלְכֵּנוּ הַגּוֹאֲלֵנוּ מִכַּף כָּל
הֶעָרִיצִים. הָאֵל הַנִּפְרָע לָנוּ
מִצָּרֵינוּ, וְהַמְשַׁלֵּם גְּמוּל
לְכָל אֹיְבֵי נַפְשֵׁנוּ, הָעֹשֶׂה
גְדֹלוֹת עַד אֵין חֵקֶר, וְנִפְלָאוֹת
עַד אֵין מִסְפָּר. הַשָּׂם נַפְשֵׁנוּ
בַּחַיִּים, וְלֹא נָתַן לַמּוֹט
רַגְלֵנוּ, הַמַּדְרִיכֵנוּ עַל בָּמוֹת
אֹיְבֵנוּ, וַיָּרֶם קַרְנֵנוּ, עַל
כָּל שׂנְאֵינוּ. הָאֵל הָעֹשֶׂה לָנוּ
נְקָמָה בְּפַרְעֹה, וְאוֹתוֹת וּמוֹפְתִים
בְּאַדְמַת בְּנֵי חָם. הַמַּכֶּה

Ve-emunöh köl zos, v'kayöm ölaynu, ki hu adonöy elohaynu v'ayn zulöso, va-anachnu yisrö-ayl amo, ha-podaynu mi-yad m'löchim, malkaynu ha-go-alaynu mikaf köl he-öri-tzim. Hö-ayl ha-nifröh lönu mitzöraynu, v'ham'shalaym g'mul l'chöl o-y'vay nafshaynu, hö-oseh g'dolos ad ayn chayker, v'niflö-os ad ayn mispör. Ha-söm nafshaynu bacha-yim, v'lo nösan lamot raglaynu, ha-madrichaynu al bömos oy'vaynu, va-yörem kar-naynu, al köl son'aynu. Hö-ayl hö-oseh lönu n'kömö b'far-oh, v'osos umof'sim b'ad'mas b'nay chöm. Ha-ma-keh

v'evröso köl b'choray mitzrö-yim,
va-yotzay es amo yisrö-ayl mi-tochöm
l'chayrus olöm. Ha-ma-avir bönöv
bayn giz'ray yam suf, v'es rod'fayhem
v'es son'ayhem bis'homos tiba,
v'rö-u vönöv g'vuröso, shib'chu
v'hodu lish'mo. Umal'chuso v'rötzon
kib'lu alayhem, mosheh uv'nay
yisro-ayl l'chö önu shirö b'simchöh
raböh, v'öm'ru chulöm.

בְּעֶבְרָתוֹ כָּל בְּכוֹרֵי מִצְרַיִם,
וַיּוֹצֵא אֶת עַמּוֹ יִשְׂרָאֵל מִתּוֹכָם
לְחֵרוּת עוֹלָם. הַמַּעֲבִיר בָּנָיו
בֵּין גִּזְרֵי יַם סוּף, וְאֶת רוֹדְפֵיהֶם
וְאֶת שׂוֹנְאֵיהֶם בִּתְהוֹמוֹת טִבַּע,
וְרָאוּ בָנָיו גְּבוּרָתוֹ, שִׁבְּחוּ
וְהוֹדוּ לִשְׁמוֹ. וּמַלְכוּתוֹ בְרָצוֹן
קִבְּלוּ עֲלֵיהֶם, מֹשֶׁה וּבְנֵי
יִשְׂרָאֵל לְךָ עָנוּ שִׁירָה בְּשִׂמְחָה
רַבָּה, וְאָמְרוּ כֻלָּם:

And belief is all this; it is established with us that He is the Lord our God, there is no other, and that we Israel are His people. It is He who redeems us from the hand of kings; our King, who delivers us from the grip of all the tyrants; the benevolent God, who avenges us against our persecutors, and brings retribution on all our mortal enemies. He does great things beyond limit, and wonders beyond number. He has kept us alive, and did not allow our feet to falter. He led us upon the high places of our foes, and increased our strength over all our adversaries. He is the benevolent God who, in our behalf, brought retribution upon Pharaoh, and signs and miracles in the land of the Hamites; who, in His wrath, struck all the first-born of Egypt and brought out His people Israel from their midst to everlasting freedom; who led His children through the divided parts of the Sea of Reeds, and drowned their pursuers and their enemies in the depths. As His children beheld His might, they extolled and offered praise to His Name, and willingly accepted His sovereignty; Moses and the children of Israel with great joy raised their voices in song to You, and they all proclaimed:

Who is Like You...   מִי כָמוֹכָה...

This prayer continues the themes of the preceding prayers. In it we proclaim the uniqueness of God, and make reference to the redemption that God has brought — and continues to bring — to the Jewish people.

מִי כָמֹכָה בָּאֵלִם יְיָ,
מִי כָּמֹכָה נֶאְדָּר בַּקֹּדֶשׁ, נוֹרָא
תְהִלֹּת, עֹשֵׂה פֶלֶא : מַלְכוּתְךָ רָאוּ
בָנֶיךָ, בּוֹקֵעַ יָם לִפְנֵי
מֹשֶׁה, זֶה אֵלִי עָנוּ וְאָמְרוּ :
יְיָ יִמְלֹךְ לְעֹלָם וָעֶד.
וְנֶאֱמַר : כִּי פָדָה יְיָ אֶת
יַעֲקֹב, וּגְאָלוֹ מִיַּד חָזָק
מִמֶּנּוּ. בָּרוּךְ אַתָּה יְיָ,
גָּאַל יִשְׂרָאֵל :

Mi chö-mochöh bö-aylim adonöy, mi kömochö ne-dör ba-kodesh, norö s'hilos, osay fe-le. Mal'chus'chö rö-u vönechö, bokay-a yöm lif'nay mosheh, zeh ayli önu v'öm'ru, adonöy yimloch l'olöm vö-ed. V'ne-emar, ki födöh adonöy es ya-akov, ug'ölo mi-yad chözök mi-menu. Böruch atöh adonöy, gö-al yisrö-ayl.

Who is like You among the supernal beings, O Lord! Who is like You, resplendent in holiness, awesome in praise, performing wonders! Your children beheld Your sovereignty as You split the sea before Moses. "This is my God!" they exclaimed, and declared, "The Lord shall reign forever and ever." And it is said: For the Lord has redeemed Jacob, and delivered him from a power mightier than he. Blessed are You Lord, who has delivered Israel.

Our Father, Let Us...

‫...הַשְׁכִּיבֵנוּ אָבִינוּ‬

It is interesting to note that in this prayer we refer to God as "Our Father," but upon waking in the morning we address Him as "Our King." The reason for this is that in the course of the day we have learned, from all that has happened to us, that God has been more than a King to us; He has shown us many kindnesses and has taken care of us like a loving father. And so, when we are about to retire for the night, we feel confident and secure in God, as a child feels secure in the arms of his father.

Hash-kivaynu övinu l'sholom,
v'ha-amidaynu malkaynu l'cha-yim
tovim ul'sholom, v'sak'naynu
b'ay-tzöh tovöh mil'fönechö,
v'hoshi-aynu m'hayröh l'ma-an
sh'mechö, uf'ros ölaynu sukas
sh'lomechö. Boruch atöh adonöy,
ha-porays sukas shölom ölaynu v'al
köl amo yisrö-ayl v'al y'rushölö-yim.

הַשְׁכִּיבֵנוּ אָבִינוּ לְשָׁלוֹם,
וְהַעֲמִידֵנוּ מַלְכֵּנוּ לְחַיִּים
טוֹבִים וּלְשָׁלוֹם, וְתַקְּנֵנוּ
בְּעֵצָה טוֹבָה מִלְּפָנֶיךָ,
וְהוֹשִׁיעֵנוּ מְהֵרָה לְמַעַן
שְׁמֶךָ, וּפְרוֹשׁ עָלֵינוּ סֻכַּת
שְׁלוֹמֶךָ. בָּרוּךְ אַתָּה יְיָ,
הַפּוֹרֵשׂ סֻכַּת שָׁלוֹם עָלֵינוּ וְעַל
כָּל עַמּוֹ יִשְׂרָאֵל וְעַל יְרוּשָׁלָיִם:

Our Father, let us lie down in peace; our King, raise us up to a good life and peace. Improve us with Your good counsel, help us speedily for the sake of Your Name, and spread over us the shelter of Your peace. Blessed are You Lord, who spreads the shelter of peace over us, over His entire people Israel, and over Jerusalem.

Leader's Half-Kaddish

חֲצִי קַדִּישׁ

The leader recites the Half-Kaddish below, followed by *Bor'chu* (Bless…).

Yis-gadal v'yis-kadash °sh'may raböh°: יִתְגַּדַּל וְיִתְקַדַּשׁ ° שְׁמֵהּ רַבָּא ° :

(Cong: Ömayn) אמן

B'öl'mö di v'rö chir'u-say בְּעָלְמָא דִּי בְרָא כִרְעוּתֵהּ

v'yamlich mal'chusay, v'yatzmach וְיַמְלִיךְ מַלְכוּתֵהּ, וְיַצְמַח

purkönay °vikörayv m'shi-chay°. פּוּרְקָנֵהּ ° וִיקָרֵב מְשִׁיחֵהּ ° :

(Cong: Ömayn) אמן

B'cha-yay-chon uv'yomaychon. בְּחַיֵּיכוֹן וּבְיוֹמֵיכוֹן

uv'chayay d'chöl bays yisrö-ayl, וּבְחַיֵּי דְכָל בֵּית יִשְׂרָאֵל,

-agölö uviz'man köriv °v'im'ru ömayn° בַּעֲגָלָא וּבִזְמַן קָרִיב ° וְאִמְרוּ אָמֵן ° :

(Cong.: Ömayn. °Y'hay sh'may rabö m'vörach אמן ° יְהֵא שְׁמֵהּ רַבָּא מְבָרַךְ

l'ölam ul'öl'may öl'ma-yöh Yisböraych°). לְעָלַם וּלְעָלְמֵי עָלְמַיָּא יִתְבָּרַךְ ° :

Yisböraych° °v'yishtabach, v'yispö-ayr, יִתְבָּרַךְ ° וְיִשְׁתַּבַּח, וְיִתְפָּאַר,

v'yisromöm, v'yis-nasay, v'yis-hadör, וְיִתְרוֹמָם, וְיִתְנַשֵּׂא, וְיִתְהַדָּר,

v'yis-aleh, v'yis-halöl°, °sh'may וְיִתְעַלֶּה, וְיִתְהַלָּל ° , ° שְׁמֵהּ

d'kud-shö b'rich hu°. דְּקֻדְשָׁא בְּרִיךְ הוּא ° :

(Cong: Ömayn) אמן

L'aylö min köl bir'chösö v'shirösö, לְעֵלָּא מִן כָּל בִּרְכָתָא וְשִׁירָתָא,

tush-b'chösö v'ne-che-mösö, תֻּשְׁבְּחָתָא וְנֶחֱמָתָא,

da-amirön b'öl'mö, °v'im'ru ömayn°. דַּאֲמִירָן בְּעָלְמָא, וְאִמְרוּ אָמֵן ° :

(Cong: Ömayn) אמן

Exalted and hallowed be His great Name (Cong: Amen.) throughout the world which He has created according to His will. May He establish His kingship, bring forth His redemption and hasten the coming of His Moshiach (Cong: Amen.) In your lifetime and in your days and in the lifetime of the entire House of Israel, speedily and soon, and say, Amen. (Cong: Amen. May His great Name be blessed forever and to all eternity. Blessed.) May His great Name be blessed forever and to all eternity. Blessed and praised, glorified, exalted and extolled, honored, adored and lauded be the Name of the Holy One, blessed be He, (Cong: Amen.) Beyond all the blessings, hymns, praises and consolations that are uttered in the world; and say, Amen.

The *Amidah*   בָּרוּךְ אַתָּה...

Recited standing, with feet together

We rise for the *Amidah*, the central prayer in which we put forth our personal requests to God. The benedictions of the Amidah are as old as our people, and date back to the times of Abraham, Isaac and Jacob. But the final form of it, as we know it in our Prayer books, dates back to a later time, that of Ezra the Scribe and the Men of the Great Assembly more than 2,300 years ago. This was during the time of the Babylonian Exile, when the Jews were driven from their land into Babylon. Many began to forget the Hebrew language. It was then that the leaders and prophets of Israel — the Men of the Great Assembly — arranged the prayers in their fixed order. Thus all the Jews, at all times and in all places would be reciting the same holy prayers, in the same language, and this would give them a feeling of unity and strength. The Sages of the Great Assembly formulated the text of the Shabbat Amidah to emphasize the sanctity and holiness of Shabbat.

What does it mean in practical terms that God sanctified the Shabbat unto His Name? It means that the Shabbat is more than a rest day, when man is to rest from his physical work; nor is it a day merely for socializing, or for ordinary enjoyment and recreation with the family. It is a day dedicated to God, a day of holiness, of prayer and of Torah study. Thus it brings a complete change from everyday life. When properly observed, on Shabbat the Jew reaches the highest degree of completeness that any creature of God can ever reach. That is why the Shabbat is the end and purpose of the entire Creation, for when man reaches that height, he "justifies" the Creation, and God is pleased with His great handiwork.

On Passover, Shavout, and Sukkot, recite the *Amidah* on page 136.

Adonöy, s'fösai tif-töch ufi
yagid t'hilö-sechö.

אֲדֹנָי, שְׂפָתַי תִּפְתָּח וּפִי
יַגִּיד תְּהִלָּתֶךָ:

My Lord, open my lips, and my mouth shall declare Your praise.

Take three steps back, then three steps forward, as if one is approaching a king. At the words *"Boruch"* (blessed), bend the knee; at *"Atoh"* (You), bow forward; and at *"Adonoy"* (Lord), straighten up.

Böruch atöh adonöy elohaynu
vay-lohay avosaynu, elohay avröhöm,
elohay yitzchök, vay-lohay ya-akov,
hö-ayl ha-gödol ha-gibör v'hanoröh,
ayl el-yon, gomayl chasödim tovim,
konay ha-kol, v'zochayr chas'day
övos, umayvi go-ayl liv-nay
v'nayhem l'ma-an sh'mo b'ahavöh.

בָּרוּךְ אַתָּה יְיָ אֱלֹהֵינוּ
וֵאלֹהֵי אֲבוֹתֵינוּ, אֱלֹהֵי אַבְרָהָם,
אֱלֹהֵי יִצְחָק, וֵאלֹהֵי יַעֲקֹב,
הָאֵל הַגָּדוֹל הַגִּבּוֹר וְהַנּוֹרָא,
אֵל עֶלְיוֹן, גּוֹמֵל חֲסָדִים טוֹבִים,
קוֹנֵה הַכֹּל, וְזוֹכֵר חַסְדֵי
אָבוֹת, וּמֵבִיא גוֹאֵל לִבְנֵי
בְנֵיהֶם לְמַעַן שְׁמוֹ בְּאַהֲבָה:

93

Between Rosh Hashana and Yom Kippur add:

Zöch'raynu l'cha-yim, melech זָכְרֵנוּ לְחַיִּים, מֶלֶךְ

chöfaytz ba-cha-yim, v'chös'vaynu חָפֵץ בַּחַיִּים, וְכָתְבֵנוּ

b'sayfer ha-cha-yim, l'ma-an'chö בְּסֵפֶר הַחַיִּים, לְמַעַנְךָ

elohim cha-yim. אֱלֹהִים חַיִּים.

At the words "*Boruch*" (blessed), bend the knee; at "*Atoh*" (You), bow forward; and at "*Adonoy*" (Lord), straighten up.

Melech ozayr umoshi-a umögayn. מֶלֶךְ עוֹזֵר וּמוֹשִׁיעַ וּמָגֵן:

Böruch atöh adonöy, בָּרוּךְ אַתָּה יְיָ,

mögayn avröhöm. מָגֵן אַבְרָהָם:

Blessed are You, Lord our God and God of our fathers, God of Abraham, God of Isaac and God of Jacob, the great, mighty and awesome God, exalted God, who bestows bountiful kindness, who creates all things, who remembers the piety of the Patriarchs, and who, in love, brings a redeemer to their children's children, for the sake of His Name. (Between Rosh Hashana and Yom Kippur add: Remember us for life, King who desires life; inscribe us in the Book of Life, for Your sake, O living God.) O King, [You are] a helper, a savior and a shield. Blessed are You Lord, Shield of Abraham.

Atöh gibor l'olöm adonöy, אַתָּה גִבּוֹר לְעוֹלָם אֲדֹנָי,

m'cha-yeh maysim atöh, rav l'hoshia. מְחַיֶּה מֵתִים אַתָּה, רַב לְהוֹשִׁיעַ:

In summer say: Morid ha-töl. בקיץ: מוֹרִיד הַטָּל:

In winter say: Mashiv höru-ach בחורף: מַשִּׁיב הָרוּחַ

u-morid ha-geshem. וּמוֹרִיד הַגֶּשֶׁם:

M'chalkayl cha-yim b'chesed,
m'cha-yeh maysim b'rachamim
rabim, somaych nof'lim, v'rofay
cholim, umatir asurim, um'ka-yaym
emunöso lishaynay öför, mi
chömochö ba-al g'vuros umi do-meh
löch, melech maymis um'cha-yeh
umatzmi-ach y'shu-öh.

מְכַלְכֵּל חַיִּים בְּחֶסֶד,
מְחַיֶּה מֵתִים בְּרַחֲמִים
רַבִּים, סוֹמֵךְ נוֹפְלִים, וְרוֹפֵא
חוֹלִים, וּמַתִּיר אֲסוּרִים, וּמְקַיֵּם
אֱמוּנָתוֹ לִישֵׁנֵי עָפָר, מִי
כָמוֹךָ בַּעַל גְּבוּרוֹת וּמִי דוֹמֶה
לָּךְ, מֶלֶךְ מֵמִית וּמְחַיֶּה
וּמַצְמִיחַ יְשׁוּעָה:

Between Rosh Hashana and Yom Kippur add:

Mi chömochö öv hörachamön zochayr
y'tzuröv l'cha-yim b'racha-mim.

מִי כָמוֹךָ אַב הָרַחֲמָן זוֹכֵר
יְצוּרָיו לְחַיִּים בְּרַחֲמִים:

V'ne-emön atöh l'ha-chayos maysim.
Boruch atöh adonöy,
m'cha-yeh ha-maysim.

וְנֶאֱמָן אַתָּה לְהַחֲיוֹת מֵתִים.
בָּרוּךְ אַתָּה יְיָ,
מְחַיֵּה הַמֵּתִים:

*You are mighty forever, my Lord; You resurrect the dead; You are powerful to save. (**In summer say:** He causes the dew to descend.) (**In winter say:** He causes the wind to blow and the rain to fall.) He sustains the living with loving-kindness, resurrects the dead with great mercy, supports the falling, heals the sick, releases the bound, and fulfills His trust to those who sleep in the dust. Who is like You, mighty One! And who can be compared to You, King, who brings death and restores life, and causes deliverance to spring forth! (**Between Rosh Hashana and Yom Kippur add:** Who is like You, merciful Father, who in compassion remembers His creatures for life.) You are trustworthy to revive the dead. Blessed are You Lord, who revives the dead.*

95

Atöh kodosh v'shim'chö kodosh	אַתָּה קָדוֹשׁ וְשִׁמְךָ קָדוֹשׁ
uk'doshim b'chöl yom y'hal'luchö	וּקְדוֹשִׁים בְּכָל יוֹם יְהַלְלוּךְ
selöh. Boruch atöh adonöy, hö-ayl	סֶלָה. בָּרוּךְ אַתָּה יְיָ, הָאֵל
ha-ködosh. (Between Rosh Hashana and	הַקָּדוֹשׁ : (בשבת שובה
Yom Kippur subsitute: Ha-melech ha-ködosh.)	הַמֶּלֶךְ הַקָּדוֹשׁ)

You are holy and Your Name is holy, and holy beings praise You daily for all eternity. Blessed are You Lord, the holy God. (Between Rosh Hashana and Yom Kippur substitute: the holy King.)

Atöh kidashtö es yom ha-sh'vi-i	אַתָּה קִדַּשְׁתָּ אֶת יוֹם הַשְּׁבִיעִי
lish'mechö, tachlis ma-asay	לִשְׁמֶךָ, תַּכְלִית מַעֲשֵׂה
shöma-yim vö-öretz, bay-rachto	שָׁמַיִם וָאָרֶץ, בֵּרַכְתּוֹ
miköl ha-yömim, v'kidashto	מִכָּל הַיָּמִים, וְקִדַּשְׁתּוֹ
miköl ha-z'manim, v'chayn	מִכָּל הַזְּמַנִּים, וְכֵן
kösuv b'sorösechö.	כָּתוּב בְּתוֹרָתֶךָ :

You have consecrated to Your Name the Seventh Day, the purpose of the creation of heaven and earth. You have blessed it above all days and sanctified it above all festivals. And thus it is written in Your Torah:

Va-y'chulu ha-shöma-yim v'hö-öretz	וַיְכֻלּוּ הַשָּׁמַיִם וְהָאָרֶץ
v'chöl tz'vö-öm. Va-y'chal elohim	וְכָל צְבָאָם : וַיְכַל אֱלֹהִים
ba-yom ha-sh'vi-i, m'lachto asher	בַּיּוֹם הַשְּׁבִיעִי, מְלַאכְתּוֹ אֲשֶׁר
ösöh, va-yishbos ba-yom ha-sh'vi-i	עָשָׂה, וַיִּשְׁבֹּת בַּיּוֹם הַשְּׁבִיעִי
miköl m'lachto asher ösöh.	מִכָּל מְלַאכְתּוֹ אֲשֶׁר עָשָׂה :
Va-y'vörech elohim es yom ha-sh'vi-i,	וַיְבָרֶךְ אֱלֹהִים אֶת יוֹם הַשְּׁבִיעִי

va-y'kadaysh oso, ki vo shövas וַיְקַדֵּשׁ אֹתוֹ, כִּי בוֹ שָׁבַת
miköl m'lachto, asher börö מִכָּל מְלַאכְתּוֹ אֲשֶׁר בָּרָא
elohim la-asos. אֱלֹהִים לַעֲשׂוֹת:

The heavens and the earth and all their hosts were completed. And God finished by the Seventh Day His work which He had done, and He rested on the Seventh Day from all His work which He had done. And God blessed the Seventh Day and made it holy, for on it He rested from all His work which God created to function.

Yis-m'chu v'mal'chus'chö shom'ray יִשְׂמְחוּ בְמַלְכוּתְךָ שׁוֹמְרֵי
shabös v'kor'ay oneg, am שַׁבָּת וְקוֹרְאֵי עֹנֶג, עַם
m'kad'shay sh'vi-i, kulöm yis-b'u מְקַדְּשֵׁי שְׁבִיעִי, כֻּלָּם יִשְׂבְּעוּ
v'yis-an'gu mituvechö, uvash'vi-i וְיִתְעַנְּגוּ מִטּוּבֶךָ, וּבַשְּׁבִיעִי
rö-tzisö bo v'kidashto, chemdas רָצִיתָ בּוֹ וְקִדַּשְׁתּוֹ, חֶמְדַּת
yömim oso körösö, zaycher יָמִים אוֹתוֹ קָרָאתָ, זֵכֶר
l'ma-asay v'rayshis. לְמַעֲשֵׂה בְרֵאשִׁית:

Those who observe the Shabbat and call it a delight shall rejoice in Your kingship; the nation which hallows the Seventh Day — all shall be satiated and delighted with Your goodness. You were pleased with the Seventh Day and made it holy; You called it the most desirable of days, in remembrance of the work of Creation.

Elohaynu vay-lohay avosay-nu, אֱלֹהֵינוּ וֵאלֹהֵי אֲבוֹתֵינוּ,
r'tzay nö vim'nuchösaynu, רְצֵה נָא בִמְנוּחָתֵנוּ,
kad'shaynu b'mitzvosechö v'sayn קַדְּשֵׁנוּ בְּמִצְוֹתֶיךָ וְתֵן

97

chel-kaynu b'sorösechö, sab'aynu   חֶלְקֵנוּ בְּתוֹרָתֶךָ, שַׂבְּעֵנוּ

mituvechö v'samay-ach naf-shaynu   מִטּוּבֶךָ וְשַׂמֵּחַ נַפְשֵׁנוּ

bishu-ösechö, v'tahayr libaynu   בִּישׁוּעָתֶךָ, וְטַהֵר לִבֵּנוּ

l'öv-d'chö be-emes, v'han-chi-laynu   לְעָבְדְּךָ בֶּאֱמֶת, וְהַנְחִילֵנוּ

adonöy elohaynu b'ahavöh   יְיָ אֱלֹהֵינוּ בְּאַהֲבָה

uv'rö-tzon shabas köd-shechö,   וּבְרָצוֹן שַׁבַּת קָדְשֶׁךָ,

v'yönuchu vöh köl yisrö-ayl   וְיָנוּחוּ בָהּ כָּל יִשְׂרָאֵל

m'kad'shay sh'mechö. Boruch atöh   מְקַדְּשֵׁי שְׁמֶךָ : בָּרוּךְ אַתָּה

adonöy, m'kadaysh ha-shabös.   יְיָ, מְקַדֵּשׁ הַשַּׁבָּת :

Our God and God of our fathers, please find favor in our rest, make us holy with Your commandments and grant us our portion in Your Torah; satiate us with Your goodness, gladden our soul with Your salvation, and make our heart pure to serve You in truth; and, Lord our God, grant as our heritage, in love and goodwill, Your holy Shabbat, and may all Israel who sanctify Your Name rest thereon. Blessed are You Lord, who sanctifies the Shabbat.

R'tzay, adonöy elohaynu, b'am'chö   רְצֵה, יְיָ אֱלֹהֵינוּ, בְּעַמְּךָ

yisrö-ayl, v'lis'filösöm sh'ay, v'höshayv   יִשְׂרָאֵל, וְלִתְפִלָּתָם שְׁעֵה, וְהָשֵׁב

hö-avodöh lid'vir bay-sechö, v'ishay   הָעֲבוֹדָה לִדְבִיר בֵּיתֶךָ, וְאִשֵּׁי

yisrö-ayl us'filösöm b'ahavöh   יִשְׂרָאֵל וּתְפִלָּתָם בְּאַהֲבָה

s'kabayl b'rö-tzon, us'hi l'rö-tzon   תְקַבֵּל בְּרָצוֹן, וּתְהִי לְרָצוֹן

tömid avodas yisrö-ayl amechö.   תָּמִיד עֲבוֹדַת יִשְׂרָאֵל עַמֶּךָ :

Look with favor, Lord our God, on Your people Israel and pay heed to their prayer; restore the service to Your Sanctuary and accept with love and favor

Israel's fire-offerings and prayer; and may the service of Your people Israel always find favor.

On Rosh Chodesh and Festivals add:

Elohaynu vay-lohay avosaynu	אֱלֹהֵינוּ וֵאלֹהֵי אֲבוֹתֵינוּ
ya-aleh v'yövo, v'yagi-a v'yayrö-eh	יַעֲלֶה וְיָבֹא, וְיַגִּיעַ וְיֵרָאֶה
v'yay-rötzeh, v'yishöma v'yipökayd	וְיֵרָצֶה, וְיִשָּׁמַע וְיִפָּקֵד
v'yizöchayr, zichro-naynu	וְיִזָּכֵר, זִכְרוֹנֵנוּ
ufik'do-naynu, v'zichron	וּפִקְדוֹנֵנוּ, וְזִכְרוֹן
avosaynu, v'zichron möshi-ach	אֲבוֹתֵינוּ, וְזִכְרוֹן מָשִׁיחַ
ben dövid avdechö, v'zichron	בֶּן דָּוִד עַבְדֶּךָ, וְזִכְרוֹן
y'rushöla-yim ir köd-shechö,	יְרוּשָׁלַיִם עִיר קָדְשֶׁךָ,
v'zichron köl am'chö bays yisrö-ayl	וְזִכְרוֹן כָּל עַמְּךָ בֵּית יִשְׂרָאֵל
l'fönechö lif'laytöh l'tovöh, l'chayn	לְפָנֶיךָ לִפְלֵיטָה לְטוֹבָה, לְחֵן
ul'chesed ul'rachamim ul'cha-yim	וּלְחֶסֶד וּלְרַחֲמִים וּלְחַיִּים
tovim ul'shölom b'yom	טוֹבִים וּלְשָׁלוֹם, בְּיוֹם

On Rosh Chodesh:	בר״ח:
rosh ha-chodesh ha-zeh.	רֹאשׁ הַחֹדֶשׁ הַזֶּה.
On Passover:	בפסח:
chag ha-matzos ha-zeh.	חַג הַמַּצּוֹת הַזֶּה.
On Sukkot:	בסוכות:
chag ha-sukos ha-zeh.	חַג הַסֻּכּוֹת הַזֶּה.

Zöch'raynu adonöy elohaynu bo	זָכְרֵנוּ יְיָ אֱלֹהֵינוּ בּוֹ
l'tovöh, ufök'daynu vo liv'röchöh	לְטוֹבָה, וּפָקְדֵנוּ בוֹ לִבְרָכָה,

99

v'hoshi-aynu vo l'cha-yim tovim.	וְהוֹשִׁיעֵנוּ בוֹ לְחַיִּים טוֹבִים :
Uvid'var y'shu-öh v'rachamim	וּבִדְבַר יְשׁוּעָה וְרַחֲמִים
chus v'chönaynu v'rachaym ölaynu	חוּס וְחָנֵּנוּ וְרַחֵם עָלֵינוּ
v'hoshi-aynu ki aylechö aynaynu,	וְהוֹשִׁיעֵנוּ כִּי אֵלֶיךָ עֵינֵינוּ,
ki ayl melech chanun	כִּי אֵל מֶלֶךְ חַנּוּן
v'rachum ötöh.	וְרַחוּם אָתָּה :

*Our God and God of our fathers, may there ascend, come and reach, be seen, accepted, and heard, recalled and remembered before You, the remembrance and recollection of us, the remembrance of our fathers, the remembrance of Moshiach the son of David Your servant, the remembrance of Jerusalem Your holy city, and the remembrance of all Your people the House of Israel, for deliverance, well-being, grace, kindness, mercy, good life and peace, on this day of: **On Rosh Chodesh:** Rosh Chodesh. **On Passover:** the Festival of Matzot. **On Sukkot:** the Festival of Sukkot. Remember us on this [day], Lord our God, for good; be mindful of us on this [day] for blessing; help us on this [day] for good life. With the promise of deliverance and compassion, spare us and be gracious to us; have mercy upon us and deliver us; for our eyes are directed to You, for You, God, are a gracious and merciful King.*

V'se-chezenöh aynaynu	וְתֶחֱזֶינָה עֵינֵינוּ
b'shuv'chö l'tziyon b'rachamim.	בְּשׁוּבְךָ לְצִיּוֹן בְּרַחֲמִים.
Böruch atöh adonöy, ha-machazir	בָּרוּךְ אַתָּה יְיָ, הַמַּחֲזִיר
sh'chinöso l'tziyon.	שְׁכִינָתוֹ לְצִיּוֹן :

May our eyes behold Your return to Zion in mercy. Blessed are You Lord, who restores His Divine Presence to Zion.

Bow forward when saying the first five words of *Modim* (We thankfully).

Modim anachnu löch, shö-atöh hu	מוֹדִים אֲנַחְנוּ לָךְ, שָׁאַתָּה הוּא
adonöy elohaynu vay-lohay avosaynu	יְיָ אֱלֹהֵינוּ וֵאלֹהֵי אֲבוֹתֵינוּ
l'olöm vö-ed, tzur cha-yaynu mögayn	לְעוֹלָם וָעֶד, צוּר חַיֵּינוּ מָגֵן
yish-aynu, atöh hu l'dor vödor,	יִשְׁעֵנוּ, אַתָּה הוּא לְדוֹר וָדוֹר,
no-deh l'chö un'sapayr t'hilösechö,	נוֹדֶה לְּךָ וּנְסַפֵּר תְּהִלָּתֶךָ,
al cha-yaynu ha-m'surim b'yödechö,	עַל חַיֵּינוּ הַמְּסוּרִים בְּיָדֶךָ,
v'al nish'mosaynu ha-p'kudos löch,	וְעַל נִשְׁמוֹתֵינוּ הַפְּקוּדוֹת לָךְ,
v'al nisechö sheb'chöl yom imönu,	וְעַל נִסֶּיךָ שֶׁבְּכָל יוֹם עִמָּנוּ,
v'al nif-l'ösechö v'tovosechö sheb'chöl	וְעַל נִפְלְאוֹתֶיךָ וְטוֹבוֹתֶיךָ שֶׁבְּכָל
ays erev vövoker v'tzöhörö-yim,	עֵת, עֶרֶב וָבֹקֶר וְצָהֳרָיִם,
ha-tov, ki lo chölu ra-chamechö,	הַטּוֹב, כִּי לֹא כָלוּ רַחֲמֶיךָ,
v'ham'rachaym, ki lo samu	וְהַמְרַחֵם, כִּי לֹא תַמּוּ
chasö-dechö, ki may-olöm kivinu löch.	חֲסָדֶיךָ, כִּי מֵעוֹלָם קִוִּינוּ לָךְ :

We thankfully acknowledge that You are the Lord our God and God of our fathers forever. You are the strength of our life, the shield of our salvation in every generation. We will give thanks to You and recount Your praise, evening, morning and noon, for our lives which are committed into Your hand, for our souls which are entrusted to You, for Your miracles which are with us daily, and for Your continual wonders and beneficences. You are the Beneficent One, for Your mercies never cease; and the Merciful One, for Your kindnesses never end; for we always place our hope in You.

During Chanukah add the following. Otherwise continue on bottom of page 103.

V'al ha-nisim v'al ha-purkön	וְעַל הַנִּסִּים וְעַל הַפֻּרְקָן
v'al ha-g'vuros v'al ha-t'shu-os	וְעַל הַגְּבוּרוֹת וְעַל הַתְּשׁוּעוֹת

v'al ha-niflö-os she-ösisö
la-avosaynu ba-yömim hö-haym
biz'man ha-zeh.

וְעַל הַנִּפְלָאוֹת שֶׁעָשִׂיתָ
לַאֲבוֹתֵינוּ בַּיָּמִים הָהֵם
בִּזְמַן הַזֶּה:

Bimay matis-yöhu ben yochönön
kohayn gödol chashmonö-i
uvönöv k'she-ö-m'döh mal'chus
yövön hör'shö-öh al
am'chö yisrö-ayl l'hashkichöm
törösechö ul'ha-aviröm
may-chukay r'tzonechö, v'atöh
b'rachamechö hörabim ömad-tö
löhem b'ays tzörösöm. Ravtö es
rivöm, dantö es dinöm, nökamtö es
nik'mösöm, mösartö giborim b'yad
chalöshim, v'rabim b'yad m'atim,
ut'may-im b'yad t'horim, ur'shö-im
b'yad tzadikim, v'zaydim b'yad
os'kay sörösechö. Ul'chö ösisö
shaym gödol v'ködosh bö-olömechö,
ul'am'chö yisrö-ayl ösisö t'shu-öh
g'dolöh ufurkön k'ha-yom ha-zeh.
V'achar kach bö-u vönechö lid'vir
bay-sechö ufinu es hay-chölechö

בִּימֵי מַתִּתְיָהוּ בֶּן יוֹחָנָן
כֹּהֵן גָּדוֹל חַשְׁמוֹנָאִי
וּבָנָיו, כְּשֶׁעָמְדָה מַלְכוּת
יָוָן הָרְשָׁעָה עַל
עַמְּךָ יִשְׂרָאֵל, לְהַשְׁכִּיחָם
תּוֹרָתֶךָ וּלְהַעֲבִירָם
מֵחֻקֵּי רְצוֹנֶךָ, וְאַתָּה
בְּרַחֲמֶיךָ הָרַבִּים עָמַדְתָּ
לָהֶם בְּעֵת צָרָתָם: רַבְתָּ אֶת
רִיבָם, דַּנְתָּ אֶת דִּינָם, נָקַמְתָּ אֶת
נִקְמָתָם, מָסַרְתָּ גִבּוֹרִים בְּיַד
חַלָּשִׁים וְרַבִּים בְּיַד מְעַטִּים
וּטְמֵאִים בְּיַד טְהוֹרִים וּרְשָׁעִים
בְּיַד צַדִּיקִים וְזֵדִים בְּיַד
עוֹסְקֵי תוֹרָתֶךָ: וּלְךָ עָשִׂיתָ
שֵׁם גָּדוֹל וְקָדוֹשׁ בָּעוֹלָמֶךָ,
וּלְעַמְּךָ יִשְׂרָאֵל עָשִׂיתָ תְּשׁוּעָה
גְדוֹלָה וּפֻרְקָן כְּהַיּוֹם הַזֶּה:
וְאַחַר כַּךְ בָּאוּ בָנֶיךָ לִדְבִיר
בֵּיתֶךָ וּפִנּוּ אֶת הֵיכָלֶךָ

v'tiharu es mik-döshechö v'hidliku וְטִהֲרוּ אֶת מִקְדָּשֶׁךָ וְהִדְלִיקוּ
nayros b'chat'zros köd-shechö, v'köv'u נֵרוֹת בְּחַצְרוֹת קָדְשֶׁךָ, וְקָבְעוּ
sh'monas y'may chanuköh aylu שְׁמוֹנַת יְמֵי חֲנֻכָּה אֵלוּ
l'hodos ul'halayl l'shim'chö ha-gödol. לְהוֹדוֹת וּלְהַלֵּל לְשִׁמְךָ הַגָּדוֹל:

And [we thank You] for the miracles, for the redemption, for the mighty deeds, for the saving acts, and for the wonders which You have wrought for our ancestors in those days, at this time — In the days of Matisyohu, the son of Yochonon the High Priest, the Hasmonean and his sons, when the wicked Hellenic government rose up against Your people Israel to make them forget Your Torah and violate the decrees of Your will. But You, in Your abounding mercies, stood by them in the time of their distress. You waged their battles, defended their rights and avenged the wrong done to them. You delivered the mighty into the hands of the weak, the many into the hands of the few, the impure into the hands of the pure, the wicked into the hands of the righteous, and the wanton sinners into the hands of those who occupy themselves with Your Torah. You made a great and holy name for Yourself in Your world, and effected a great deliverance and redemption for Your people to this very day. Then Your children entered the shrine of Your House, cleansed Your Temple, purified Your Sanctuary, kindled lights in Your holy courtyards, and instituted these eight days of Chanukah to give thanks and praise to Your great Name.

V'al kulöm yis-böraych v'yisromöm וְעַל כֻּלָּם יִתְבָּרֵךְ וְיִתְרוֹמָם
v'yisnasay shim'chö malkaynu וְיִתְנַשֵּׂא שִׁמְךָ מַלְכֵּנוּ
tömid l'olöm vö-ed. תָּמִיד לְעוֹלָם וָעֶד:

And for all these, may Your Name, our King, be continually blessed, exalted and extolled forever and all time.

103

Between Rosh Hashana and Yom Kippur add:

Uch'sov l'cha-yim tovim   וּכְתוֹב לְחַיִּים טוֹבִים
köl b'nay v'risechö.   כָּל בְּנֵי בְרִיתֶךָ:

Inscribe all the children of Your Covenant for a good life.

At the words *"Boruch"* (blessed), bend the knee; at *"Atoh"* (You), bow forward; and at *"Adonoy"* (Lord), straighten up.

V'chöl ha-cha-yim yo-duchö selöh   וְכָל הַחַיִּים יוֹדוּךָ סֶּלָה
vihal'lu shim'chö ha-gödol l'olöm ki   וִיהַלְלוּ שִׁמְךָ הַגָּדוֹל לְעוֹלָם כִּי
tov, hö-ayl y'shu-ösaynu v'ezrösaynu   טוֹב, הָאֵל יְשׁוּעָתֵנוּ וְעֶזְרָתֵנוּ
selöh, hö-ayl ha-tov. Boruch atöh   סֶּלָה, הָאֵל הַטּוֹב. בָּרוּךְ אַתָּה
adonöy, ha-tov shim'chö ul'chö   יְיָ, הַטּוֹב שִׁמְךָ וּלְךָ
nö-eh l'hodos.   נָאֶה לְהוֹדוֹת:

And all living things shall forever thank You, and praise Your great Name eternally, for You are good. God, You are our everlasting salvation and help, O benevolent God. Blessed are You Lord, Beneficent is Your Name, and to You it is fitting to offer thanks.

Sim shölom tovöh uv'röchöh,   שִׂים שָׁלוֹם, טוֹבָה וּבְרָכָה,
cha-yim chayn vöchesed v'rachamim,   חַיִּים חֵן וָחֶסֶד וְרַחֲמִים,
ölaynu v'al köl yisrö-ayl amechö.   עָלֵינוּ וְעַל כָּל יִשְׂרָאֵל עַמֶּךָ.
Bö-r'chaynu övinu kulönu k'echöd   בָּרְכֵנוּ אָבִינוּ כֻּלָּנוּ כְּאֶחָד,
b'or pönechö, ki v'or pönechö,   בְּאוֹר פָּנֶיךָ, כִּי בְאוֹר פָּנֶיךָ,
nösatö lönu, adonöy elohaynu,   נָתַתָּ לָנוּ יְיָ אֱלֹהֵינוּ,
toras cha-yim v'ahavas chesed   תּוֹרַת חַיִּים, וְאַהֲבַת חֶסֶד
utz'dököh uv'röchöh v'rachamim   וּצְדָקָה וּבְרָכָה וְרַחֲמִים

v'cha-yim v'shölom. V'tov b'aynechö
l'vöraych es am'chö yisrö-ayl b'chöl
ays uv'chöl shö-öh bish'lomechö.

וְחַיִּים וְשָׁלוֹם. וְטוֹב בְּעֵינֶיךָ
לְבָרֵךְ אֶת עַמְּךָ יִשְׂרָאֵל בְּכָל
עֵת וּבְכָל שָׁעָה בִּשְׁלוֹמֶךָ.

Bestow peace, goodness and blessing, life, graciousness, kindness and mercy, upon us and upon all Your people Israel. Bless us, our Father, all of us as one, with the light of Your countenance. For by the light of Your countenance You gave us, Lord our God, the Torah of life and loving-kindness, righteousness, blessing, mercy, life and peace. May it be favorable in Your eyes to bless Your people Israel, at all times and at every moment, with Your peace.

Between Rosh Hashana and Yom Kippur add:

Uv'sayfer cha-yim b'röchöh
v'shölom ufarnösöh tovöh,
y'shu-öh v'nechömöh, ug'zayros
tovos, nizöchayr v'nikösayv
l'fönechö, anachnu v'chöl am'chö
bays yisrö-ayl, l'cha-yim
tovim ul'shölom.

וּבְסֵפֶר חַיִּים בְּרָכָה
וְשָׁלוֹם וּפַרְנָסָה טוֹבָה
יְשׁוּעָה וְנֶחָמָה וּגְזֵרוֹת
טוֹבוֹת נִזָּכֵר וְנִכָּתֵב
לְפָנֶיךָ, אֲנַחְנוּ וְכָל עַמְּךָ
בֵּית יִשְׂרָאֵל, לְחַיִּים
טוֹבִים וּלְשָׁלוֹם.

And in the Book of Life, blessing, peace and prosperity, deliverance, consolation and favorable decrees, may we and all Your people the House of Israel be remembered and inscribed before You for a happy life and for peace.

Boruch atöh adonöy, ha-m'vöraych es
amo yisrö-ayl ba-shölom.

בָּרוּךְ אַתָּה יְיָ, הַמְבָרֵךְ אֶת
עַמּוֹ יִשְׂרָאֵל בַּשָּׁלוֹם:

Blessed are You Lord, who blesses His people Israel with peace.

Yih-yu l'rö-tzon im'ray fi, v'heg-yon
libi l'fönechö, adonöy tzuri v'go-ali.

יִהְיוּ לְרָצוֹן אִמְרֵי פִי, וְהֶגְיוֹן
לִבִּי לְפָנֶיךָ, יְיָ צוּרִי וְגוֹאֲלִי.

*May the words of my mouth and the meditation of my heart be acceptable
before You, Lord, my Strength and my Redeemer.*

Elohai, n'tzor l'shoni may-rö, us'fösai
midabayr mirmöh. V'lim'kal'lai,
nafshi sidom, v'nafshi ke-öför la-kol
tih-yeh. P'sach libi b'sorösechö,
uv'mitzvosechö tirdof nafshi,
v'chöl ha-chosh'vim ölai rö-öh,
m'hayröh höfayr atzösöm v'kalkayl
ma-chashavtöm. Yih-yu k'motz lif'nay
ru-ach umal'ach adonöy do-cheh.
L'ma-an yay-chöl'tzun y'didechö,
hoshi-öh y'min'chö va-anayni.
Asay l'ma-an sh'mechö, asay l'ma-an
y'minechö, asay l'ma-an torösechö,
asay l'ma-an k'dusho-sechö.

אֱלֹהַי, נְצוֹר לְשׁוֹנִי מֵרָע, וּשְׂפָתַי
מִדַּבֵּר מִרְמָה: וְלִמְקַלְלַי,
נַפְשִׁי תִדּוֹם, וְנַפְשִׁי כֶּעָפָר לַכֹּל
תִּהְיֶה: פְּתַח לִבִּי בְּתוֹרָתֶךָ,
וּבְמִצְוֹתֶיךָ תִּרְדּוֹף נַפְשִׁי,
וְכָל הַחוֹשְׁבִים עָלַי רָעָה,
מְהֵרָה הָפֵר עֲצָתָם וְקַלְקֵל
מַחֲשַׁבְתָּם: יִהְיוּ כְּמוֹץ לִפְנֵי
רוּחַ וּמַלְאַךְ יְיָ דּוֹחֶה:
לְמַעַן יֵחָלְצוּן יְדִידֶיךָ,
הוֹשִׁיעָה יְמִינְךָ וַעֲנֵנִי:
עֲשֵׂה לְמַעַן שְׁמֶךָ, עֲשֵׂה לְמַעַן
יְמִינֶךָ, עֲשֵׂה לְמַעַן תּוֹרָתֶךָ:
עֲשֵׂה לְמַעַן קְדֻשָּׁתֶךָ:

Yih-yu l'rö-tzon im'ray fi, v'heg-yon
libi l'fönechö, adonöy tzuri v'go-ali.

יִהְיוּ לְרָצוֹן אִמְרֵי פִי, וְהֶגְיוֹן
לִבִּי לְפָנֶיךָ, יְיָ צוּרִי וְגוֹאֲלִי.

*My God, guard my tongue from evil and my lips from speaking deceitfully. Let
my soul be silent to those who curse me; let my soul be as dust to all. Open my*

heart to Your Torah, and let my soul eagerly pursue Your commandments. As for all those who plot evil against me, hasten to annul their counsel and frustrate their design. Let them be as chaff before the wind; let the angel of the Lord thrust them away. That Your beloved ones may be delivered, help with Your right hand and answer me. Do it for the sake of Your Name; do it for the sake of Your right hand; do it for the sake of Your Torah; do it for the sake of Your holiness. May the words of my mouth and the meditation of my heart be acceptable before You, Lord, my Strength and my Redeemer.

Take three steps back and say:

עֹשֶׂה שָׁלוֹם (בש״ת: הַשָּׁלוֹם)   O-seh shölom (**Between Rosh Hashana**
בִּמְרוֹמָיו, הוּא יַעֲשֶׂה   **and Yom Kippur:** ha-shölom) bim'romöv,
שָׁלוֹם עָלֵינוּ וְעַל כָּל   hu ya-aseh shölom ölaynu v'al köl
יִשְׂרָאֵל, וְאִמְרוּ אָמֵן :   yisrö-ayl, v'im'ru ömayn.

*He who makes peace (**Between Rosh Hashana and Yom Kippur substitute:** the peace) in His heavens, may He make peace for us and for all Israel; and say: Amen.*

יְהִי רָצוֹן מִלְּפָנֶיךָ, יְיָ   Y'hi rö-tzon mil'fönechö, adonöy
אֱלֹהֵינוּ וֵאלֹהֵי אֲבוֹתֵינוּ,   elohaynu vay-löhay avosaynu,
שֶׁיִּבָּנֶה בֵּית הַמִּקְדָּשׁ   she-yibö-neh bays ha-mikdösh
בִּמְהֵרָה בְיָמֵינוּ, וְתֵן   bim'hayröh v'yömaynu, v'sayn
חֶלְקֵנוּ בְּתוֹרָתֶךָ :   chelkaynu b'sorösechö.

May it be Your will, Lord our God and God of our fathers, that the Beit Hamikdash (Holy Temple) be speedily rebuilt in our days, and grant us our portion in Your Torah.

Take three steps forward. This concludes the *Amidah*.

107

The Heavens... וַיְכֻלּוּ הַשָּׁמַיִם...

Recited standing

These verses are from the first chapter in Genesis. By reciting them a Jew gives testimony that God created the heavens and the earth and all that is in them — in six days, and rested on the seventh, which He proclaimed a holy day of rest. Every Jew should realize the great and unique privilege to be such a witness. Hence the book of the *Zohar* (kabbalah) concludes: "A Jew should give this testimony with joy and gladness of heart."

וַיְכֻלּוּ הַשָּׁמַיִם וְהָאָרֶץ
Va-y'chulu ha-shöma-yim v'hö-öretz

וְכָל צְבָאָם: וַיְכַל אֱלֹהִים
v'chöl tz'vö-öm. Va-y'chal elohim

בַּיּוֹם הַשְּׁבִיעִי, מְלַאכְתּוֹ אֲשֶׁר
ba-yom ha-sh'vi-i, m'lachto asher

עָשָׂה, וַיִּשְׁבֹּת בַּיּוֹם הַשְּׁבִיעִי
ösöh, va-yishbos ba-yom ha-sh'vi-i

מִכָּל מְלַאכְתּוֹ אֲשֶׁר עָשָׂה:
miköl m'lachto asher ösöh.

וַיְבָרֶךְ אֱלֹהִים אֶת יוֹם הַשְּׁבִיעִי
Va-y'vörech elohim es yom ha-sh'vi-i,

וַיְקַדֵּשׁ אֹתוֹ, כִּי בוֹ שָׁבַת
va-y'kadaysh oso, ki vo shövas

מִכָּל מְלַאכְתּוֹ אֲשֶׁר בָּרָא
miköl m'lachto, asher börö

אֱלֹהִים לַעֲשׂוֹת:
elohim la-asos.

The heavens and the earth and all their hosts were completed. And God finished by the Seventh Day His work which He had done, and He rested on the Seventh Day from all His work which He had done. And God blessed the Seventh Day and made it holy, for on it He rested from all His work which God created to function.

When praying with a *Minyan*, the leader recites the following blessing:

Böruch atöh adonöy elohaynu
vay-lohay avosaynu, elohay avröhöm,
elohay yitzchök, vay-lohay ya-akov,
hö-ayl ha-gödol ha-gibör v'ha-noröh
ayl el-yon, konay shöma-yim vö-retz.

בָּרוּךְ אַתָּה יְיָ, אֱלֹהֵינוּ
וֵאלֹהֵי אֲבוֹתֵינוּ, אֱלֹהֵי אַבְרָהָם,
אֱלֹהֵי יִצְחָק, וֵאלֹהֵי יַעֲקֹב,
הָאֵל הַגָּדוֹל הַגִּבּוֹר וְהַנּוֹרָא
אֵל עֶלְיוֹן קוֹנֵה שָׁמַיִם וָאָרֶץ :

Blessed are You, Lord our God and God of our fathers, God of Abraham, God of Isaac and God of Jacob, the great, mighty and awesome God, exalted God, Creator of heaven and earth.

He Was a Shield...

מָגֵן אָבוֹת...

The words "He was a shield," "He resurrects the dead" and "the holy King" clearly refer to the familiar first three blessings of the *Amidah*. The words "for to them He decided to give rest" refer to the central Shabbat blessing, "please find favor in our rest." The words "We will serve Him," "God worthy of praise" and "Master of Peace" refer to the familiar last three blessings of every *Amidah*.

Mögayn övos bid'võro m'cha-yeh
maysim b'ma-amöro hö-ayl (bet. Rosh
Hashana and Yom Kippur substitute: ha-melech)
ha-ködosh she-ayn kömohu
ha-mayni-ach l'amo b'yom shabbas

מָגֵן אָבוֹת בִּדְבָרוֹ מְחַיֶּה
מֵתִים בְּמַאֲמָרוֹ הָאֵל
(בש״ת הַמֶּלֶךְ)
הַקָּדוֹשׁ שֶׁאֵין כָּמוֹהוּ
הַמֵּנִיחַ לְעַמּוֹ בְּיוֹם שַׁבָּת

109

köd-sho, ki vöm rötzöh l'höni-ach   קָדְשׁוֹ, כִּי בָם רָצָה לְהָנִיחַ

löhem, l'fönöv na-avod b'yir-öh   לָהֶם, לְפָנָיו נַעֲבוֹד בְּיִרְאָה

vö-fachad v'no-deh lish'mo b'chöl   וָפַחַד וְנוֹדֶה לִשְׁמוֹ בְּכָל

yom tömid, may-ayn ha-b'röchos,   יוֹם תָּמִיד, מֵעֵין הַבְּרָכוֹת,

ayl ha-hodö-os adon ha-shölom,   אֵל הַהוֹדָאוֹת אֲדוֹן הַשָּׁלוֹם,

m'kadaysh ha-shabös um'vöraych   מְקַדֵּשׁ הַשַּׁבָּת וּמְבָרֵךְ

sh'vi-i, umayni-ach bik'dushöh,   שְׁבִיעִי, וּמֵנִיחַ בִּקְדֻשָּׁה,

l'am m'dush'nay oneg, zaycher   לְעַם מְדֻשְּׁנֵי עֹנֶג, זֵכֶר

l'ma-asay v'rayshis.   לְמַעֲשֵׂה בְרֵאשִׁית:

He was a shield to our fathers with His word; He resurrects the dead by His utterance; He is the holy God (**Between Rosh Hashana and Yom Kippur substitute:** *the holy King*) *like whom there is none. He gives rest to His people on His holy Shabbat day, for to them He desired to give rest. We will serve Him with awe and fear, and offer thanks to His Name every day, continually, in accordance with the blessings [of that day]. He is the God worthy of thanks, the Master of peace, who sanctifies the Shabbat and blesses the Seventh Day and brings rest with holiness to a people satiated with delight — in remembrance of the work of Creation.*

When praying with a *Minyan*, the leader recites the following:

Elohaynu vay-lo-hay avosay-nu,   אֱלֹהֵינוּ וֵאלֹהֵי אֲבוֹתֵינוּ,

r'tzay nö vim'nuchösaynu,   רְצֵה נָא בִמְנוּחָתֵנוּ,

kad'shaynu b'mitzvosechö v'sayn   קַדְּשֵׁנוּ בְּמִצְוֹתֶיךָ וְתֵן

chel-kaynu b'sorösechö, sab'aynu   חֶלְקֵנוּ בְּתוֹרָתֶךָ, שַׂבְּעֵנוּ

mi-tuvechö v'samay-ach nafshaynu   מִטּוּבֶךָ וְשַׂמֵּחַ נַפְשֵׁנוּ

bishu-ösechö, v'tahayr libaynu	בִּישׁוּעָתֶךָ, וְטַהֵר לִבֵּנוּ
l'öv-d'chö be-emes, v'han-chi-laynu	לְעָבְדְּךָ בֶּאֱמֶת, וְהַנְחִילֵנוּ
adonöy elohaynu b'ahavöh	יְיָ אֱלֹהֵינוּ בְּאַהֲבָה
uv'rö-tzon shabas köd-shechö,	וּבְרָצוֹן שַׁבַּת קָדְשֶׁךָ,
v'yönuchu vöh köl yisrö-ayl	וְיָנוּחוּ בָהּ כָּל יִשְׂרָאֵל
m'kad'shay sh'mechö. Boruch atöh	מְקַדְּשֵׁי שְׁמֶךָ: בָּרוּךְ אַתָּה
adonöy, m'kadaysh ha-shabös.	יְיָ, מְקַדֵּשׁ הַשַּׁבָּת:

*Our God and God of our fathers, please find favor in our rest, make us holy
with Your commandments and grant us our portion in Your Torah; satiate us
with Your goodness, gladden our soul with Your salvation, and make our heart
pure to serve You in truth; and, Lord our God, grant as our heritage, in love
and goodwill, Your holy Shabbat, and may all Israel who sanctify Your Name
rest thereon. Blessed are You Lord, who sanctifies the Shabbat.*

Leader's Whole Kaddish קַדִּישׁ שָׁלֵם

When praying with a *Minyan*, the leader recites whole kaddish

Yis-gadal v'yis-kadash °sh'may raböh°:	יִתְגַּדַּל וְיִתְקַדַּשׁ °שְׁמֵהּ רַבָּא°:
(Cong: Ömayn)	אמן
B'öl'mö di v'rö chir'u-say	בְּעָלְמָא דִּי בְרָא כִרְעוּתֵהּ
v'yamlich mal'chusay, v'yatzmach	וְיַמְלִיךְ מַלְכוּתֵהּ, וְיַצְמַח
purkönay °vikörayv m'shi-chay°:	פּוּרְקָנֵהּ °וִיקָרֵב מְשִׁיחֵהּ°:
(Cong: Ömayn)	אמן

111

B'cha-yay-chon uv'yomaychon.   בְּחַיֵּיכוֹן וּבְיוֹמֵיכוֹן

uv'chayay d'chöl bays yisrö-ayl,   וּבְחַיֵּי דְכָל בֵּית יִשְׂרָאֵל,

-agölö uviz'man köriv °v'im'ru ömayn°   בַּעֲגָלָא וּבִזְמַן קָרִיב וְאִמְרוּ אָמֵן°:

(Cong.: Ömayn. °Y'hay sh'may rabö m'vörach   אמן °יְהֵא שְׁמֵהּ רַבָּא מְבָרַךְ

l'ölam ul'öl'may öl'ma-yöh Yisböraych°).   לְעָלַם וּלְעָלְמֵי עָלְמַיָּא יִתְבָּרַךְ°:

Yisböraych° °v'yishtabach, v'yispö-ayr,   יִתְבָּרַךְ°, °וְיִשְׁתַּבַּח, וְיִתְפָּאַר,

v'yisromöm, v'yis-nasay, v'yis-hadör,   וְיִתְרוֹמָם, וְיִתְנַשֵּׂא, וְיִתְהַדָּר,

v'yis-aleh, v'yis-halöl°, °sh'may   וְיִתְעַלֶּה, וְיִתְהַלָּל°, °שְׁמֵהּ

d'kud-shö b'rich hu°.   דְּקֻדְשָׁא בְּרִיךְ הוּא°:

(Cong: Ömayn)   אמן

L'aylö min köl bir'chösö v'shirösö,   לְעֵלָּא מִן כָּל בִּרְכָתָא וְשִׁירָתָא,

tush-b'chösö v'ne-che-mösö,   תֻּשְׁבְּחָתָא וְנֶחֱמָתָא,

da-amirön b'öl'mö, °v'im'ru ömayn°.   דַּאֲמִירָן בְּעָלְמָא, וְאִמְרוּ אָמֵן°:

(Cong: Ömayn)   אמן

Tiskabayl tz'los-hon uvö-us-hon   תִּתְקַבֵּל צְלוֹתְהוֹן וּבָעוּתְהוֹן

d'chöl bays yisrö-ayl, ködöm avu-hon   דְכָל בֵּית יִשְׂרָאֵל, קֳדָם אֲבוּהוֹן

di vish'ma-yö, °v'im'ru ömayn°.   דִּי בִשְׁמַיָּא, °וְאִמְרוּ אָמֵן°:

(Cong: Ömayn)   אמן

Y'hay sh'lömö rabö min sh'ma-yö,   יְהֵא שְׁלָמָא רַבָּא מִן שְׁמַיָּא

v'cha-yim tovim ölaynu v'al köl   וְחַיִּים טוֹבִים עָלֵינוּ וְעַל כָּל

yisrö-ayl °v'im'ru ömayn°.   יִשְׂרָאֵל °וְאִמְרוּ אָמֵן°:

(Cong: Ömayn)   אמן

>O-seh shölom (Between Rosh Hashana   ‹עֹשֶׂה שָׁלוֹם

and Yom Kippur substitute: ha-shölom)   (בעשי״ת: הַשָּׁלוֹם)

bim'romöv, ^hu <ya-aseh sholom
ölaynu ^v'al köl yisrö-ayl,
°v'im'ru ömayn°. (Cong: Ömayn)

בִּמְרוֹמָיו, ^ הוּא <יַעֲשֶׂה
שָׁלוֹם עָלֵינוּ ^וְעַל כָּל יִשְׂרָאֵל,
°וְאִמְרוּ אָמֵן°: אמן

A Psalm By David...

מִזְמוֹר לְדָוִד...

Recited standing

This Psalm is one of the most familiar of the Book of Psalms. It is also one of the most beautiful and comforting. The whole serene picture of peace and comfort, free from anxiety and fear, plus a feeling of closeness to God — all this reflects the Shabbat atmosphere.

Mizmor l'dövid, adonöy ro-i lo
echsör. Bin'os deshe yarbi-tzayni,
al may m'nuchos y'nahalayni. Nafshi
y'shovayv, yan-chayni v'ma-g'lay
tzedek l'ma-an sh'mo. Gam ki aylech
b'gay tzalmöves lo irö rö, ki
atöh imödi, shiv-t'chö umish-antechö
haymöh y'nachamuni. Ta-aroch
l'fönai shulchön neged tzo-r'röy,
dishantö vashemen roshi,
kosi r'vö-yöh. Ach tov vöchesed
yir-d'funi köl y'may cha-yöy, v'shavti
b'vays adonöy l'orech yömim.

מִזְמוֹר לְדָוִד, יְיָ רֹעִי לֹא
אֶחְסָר: בִּנְאוֹת דֶּשֶׁא יַרְבִּיצֵנִי,
עַל מֵי מְנֻחוֹת יְנַהֲלֵנִי: נַפְשִׁי
יְשׁוֹבֵב, יַנְחֵנִי בְמַעְגְּלֵי
צֶדֶק לְמַעַן שְׁמוֹ: גַּם כִּי אֵלֵךְ
בְּגֵיא צַלְמָוֶת לֹא אִירָא רָע, כִּי
אַתָּה עִמָּדִי, שִׁבְטְךָ וּמִשְׁעַנְתֶּךָ
הֵמָּה יְנַחֲמֻנִי: תַּעֲרֹךְ
לְפָנַי שֻׁלְחָן נֶגֶד צֹרְרָי,
דִּשַּׁנְתָּ בַשֶּׁמֶן רֹאשִׁי,
כּוֹסִי רְוָיָה: אַךְ טוֹב וָחֶסֶד
יִרְדְּפוּנִי כָּל יְמֵי חַיָּי, וְשַׁבְתִּי
בְּבֵית יְיָ לְאֹרֶךְ יָמִים:

A Psalm by David. The Lord is my shepherd; I shall lack nothing. He makes me lie down in green pastures; He leads me beside still waters. He revives my soul; He directs me in the paths of righteousness for the sake of His Name. Even if I will walk in the valley of the shadow of death, I will fear no evil, for You are with me; Your rod and Your staff — they will comfort me. You will prepare a table for me before my enemies; You have anointed my head with oil; my cup is full. Only goodness and kindness shall follow me all the days of my life, and I shall dwell in the House of the Lord for many long years.

Leader's Half Kaddish... חֲצִי_קַדִּישׁ

The leader recites half kaddish, followed by *Bor'chu* (Bless...).

Yis-gadal v'yis-kadash °sh'may raböh°:	יִתְגַּדַּל וְיִתְקַדַּשׁ ∘שְׁמֵהּ רַבָּא∘:
(Cong: Ömayn)	אמן
B'öl'mö di v'rö chir'u-say	בְּעָלְמָא דִּי בְרָא כִרְעוּתֵהּ
v'yamlich mal'chusay, v'yatzmach	וְיַמְלִיךְ מַלְכוּתֵהּ, וְיַצְמַח
purkönay °vikörayv m'shi-chay°.	פּוּרְקָנֵהּ ∘וִיקָרֵב מְשִׁיחֵהּ∘:
(Cong: Ömayn)	אמן
B'cha-yay-chon uv'yomaychon.	בְּחַיֵּיכוֹן וּבְיוֹמֵיכוֹן
uv'chayay d'chöl bays yisrö-ayl,	וּבְחַיֵּי דְכָל בֵּית יִשְׂרָאֵל,
-agölö uviz'man köriv °v'im'ru ömayn°	בַּעֲגָלָא וּבִזְמַן קָרִיב ∘וְאִמְרוּ אָמֵן∘:
(Cong.: Ömayn. °Y'hay sh'may rabö m'vörach	אמן ∘יְהֵא שְׁמֵהּ רַבָּא מְבָרַךְ
l'ölam ul'öl'may öl'ma-yöh Yisböraych°).	לְעָלַם וּלְעָלְמֵי עָלְמַיָּא יִתְבָּרַךְ:
Yisböraych° °v'yishtabach, v'yispö-ayr,	יִתְבָּרַךְ∘ ∘וְיִשְׁתַּבַּח, וְיִתְפָּאַר,
v'yisromöm, v'yis-nasay, v'yis-hadör,	וְיִתְרוֹמָם, וְיִתְנַשֵּׂא, וְיִתְהַדָּר,

114

v'yis-aleh, v'yis-halöl°, °sh'may שְׁמֵהּ °וְיִתְעַלֶּה, וְיִתְהַלָּל°,
d'kud-shö b'rich hu°. דְּקֻדְשָׁא בְּרִיךְ הוּא°:

(Cong: Ömayn) אמן

L'aylö min köl bir'chöso v'shiröso, לְעֵלָּא מִן כָּל בִּרְכָתָא וְשִׁירָתָא,
tush-b'chöso v'ne-che-möso, תֻּשְׁבְּחָתָא וְנֶחֱמָתָא,
da-amirön b'öl'mö, °v'im'ru ömayn°. דַּאֲמִירָן בְּעָלְמָא, °וְאִמְרוּ אָמֵן°:

(Cong: Ömayn) אמן

Bor'chu is recited standing. When saying the words, we bow in reverence to God.

Leader: חזן:
Bö-r'chu es adonöy ha-m'voröch. בָּרְכוּ אֶת יְיָ הַמְבֹרָךְ:

Congregation and leader: קהל וחזן:
Böruch adonöy ha-m'voröch בָּרוּךְ יְיָ הַמְבֹרָךְ
l'olöm vö-ed. לְעוֹלָם וָעֶד:

Leader: *Bless the Lord who is blessed.* Congregation and Leader: *Blessed be the Lord who is blessed for all eternity.*

From the second night of Passover until the night before Shavuot, the *Omer* is counted here (see page 127). Otherwise continue below.

115

It is Incumbent...

עָלֵינוּ...

Recited standing.

Our Sages tell us that this prayer was composed by Joshua, as he led the children of Israel into the Promised Land. And if you look carefully you will find that the initials taken from the first letter of each sentence in the first paragraph, read backwards, form his name "Hoshua." Thus, when Joshua was about to settle the Jewish people in the Holy Land, he made them remember, through this hymn, that they were different from the Canaanite peoples and other nations and tribes of the earth, who "worship vain things and emptiness."

Ölaynu l'shabay-ach la-adon ha-kol, עָלֵינוּ לְשַׁבֵּחַ לַאֲדוֹן הַכֹּל,

lösays g'dulöh l'yo-tzayr b'rayshis, לָתֵת גְּדֻלָּה לְיוֹצֵר בְּרֵאשִׁית,

shelo ösönu k'go-yay hö-arötzos, v'lo שֶׁלֹּא עָשָׂנוּ כְּגוֹיֵי הָאֲרָצוֹת, וְלֹא

sömonu k'mish-p'chos hö-adömöh, שָׂמָנוּ כְּמִשְׁפְּחוֹת הָאֲדָמָה,

shelo söm chelkaynu köhem, שֶׁלֹּא שָׂם חֶלְקֵנוּ כָּהֶם,

v'gorölaynu k'chöl ha-monöm וְגֹרָלֵנוּ כְּכָל הֲמוֹנָם

she-haym mishtachavim l'hevel v'lörik. שֶׁהֵם מִשְׁתַּחֲוִים לְהֶבֶל וְלָרִיק.

Va-anachnu kor'im umi-shtachavim וַאֲנַחְנוּ כּוֹרְעִים וּמִשְׁתַּחֲוִים

umodim, lif'nay melech, mal'chay וּמוֹדִים, לִפְנֵי מֶלֶךְ, מַלְכֵי

ha-m'löchim, ha-ködosh böruch הַמְּלָכִים, הַקָּדוֹשׁ בָּרוּךְ

hu. She-hu noteh shöma-yim הוּא. שֶׁהוּא נוֹטֶה שָׁמַיִם

v'yosayd ö-retz, umoshav y'köro וְיוֹסֵד אָרֶץ, וּמוֹשַׁב יְקָרוֹ

בַּשָּׁמַיִם מִמַּעַל, וּשְׁכִינַת ba-shöma-yim mima-al, ush'chinas

עֻזּוֹ בְּגָבְהֵי מְרוֹמִים, הוּא אֱלֹהֵינוּ uzo b'göv'hay m'romim, hu elohaynu

אֵין עוֹד. אֱמֶת מַלְכֵּנוּ, אֶפֶס ayn od. Emes malkaynu, efes

זוּלָתוֹ, כַּכָּתוּב בְּתוֹרָתוֹ: וְיָדַעְתָּ zulöso, kakösuv b'soröso: V'yöda-tö

הַיּוֹם וַהֲשֵׁבֹתָ אֶל לְבָבֶךָ, ha-yom va-hashay-vosö el l'vövechö,

כִּי יְיָ הוּא הָאֱלֹהִים בַּשָּׁמַיִם ki adonöy hu hö-elohim ba-shöma-yim

מִמַּעַל, וְעַל הָאָרֶץ mima-al, v'al hö-öretz

מִתָּחַת, אֵין עוֹד: mi-töchas, ayn od.

It is incumbent upon us to praise the Master of all things, to exalt the Creator of all existence, that He has not made us like the nations of the world, nor caused us to be like the families of the earth; that He has not assigned us a portion like theirs, nor a lot like that of all their multitudes, for they bow to vanity and nothingness. But we bend the knee, bow down, and offer praise before the supreme King of kings, the Holy One, blessed be He, who stretches forth the heavens and establishes the earth, the seat of whose glory is in the heavens above and the abode of whose majesty is in the loftiest heights. He is our God; there is none else. Truly, He is our King; there is nothing besides Him, as it is written in His Torah: Know this day and take unto your heart that the Lord is God; in the heavens above and upon the earth below there is nothing else.

וְעַל כֵּן נְקַוֶּה לְךָ יְיָ V'al kayn n'ka-veh l'chö adonöy

אֱלֹהֵינוּ, לִרְאוֹת מְהֵרָה elohaynu, lir-os m'hayröh

בְּתִפְאֶרֶת עֻזֶּךָ, לְהַעֲבִיר גִּלּוּלִים b'sif-eres uzechö, l'ha-avir gilulim

מִן הָאָרֶץ וְהָאֱלִילִים כָּרוֹת min hö-öretz v'hö-elilim köros

יִכָּרֵתוּן, לְתַקֵּן עוֹלָם yiköray-sun, l'sakayn olöm

b'mal'chus shadai, v'chöl b'nay vösör
yik-r'u vish'mechö, l'hafnos ay-lechö
köl rish'ay öretz. Yakiru v'yay-d'u köl
yosh'vay sayvayl, ki l'chö tichra köl
berech, tishöva köl löshon. L'fönechö
adonöy elohaynu yich-r'u v'yipolu,
v'lich'vod shim'chö y'kör yitaynu,
vi-kab'lu chulöm alay-hem es ol
mal'chusechö, v'simloch alayhem
m'hayröh l'olöm vö-ed, ki
ha-mal'chus shel'chö hi, ul'ol'may ad
timloch b'chövod, ka-kösuv
b'sorösechö, adonöy yimloch l'olöm
vö-ed. V'ne-emar, v'hö-yöh adonöy
l'melech al köl hö-öretz, ba-yom
hahu yih-yeh adonöy echöd
ush'mo echöd.

בְּמַלְכוּת שַׁדַּי, וְכָל בְּנֵי בָשָׂר
יִקְרְאוּ בִשְׁמֶךָ, לְהַפְנוֹת אֵלֶיךָ
כָּל רִשְׁעֵי אָרֶץ. יַכִּירוּ וְיֵדְעוּ כָּל
יוֹשְׁבֵי תֵבֵל, כִּי לְךָ תִּכְרַע כָּל
בֶּרֶךְ, תִּשָּׁבַע כָּל לָשׁוֹן. לְפָנֶיךָ
יְיָ אֱלֹהֵינוּ יִכְרְעוּ וְיִפּוֹלוּ,
וְלִכְבוֹד שִׁמְךָ יְקָר יִתֵּנוּ,
וִיקַבְּלוּ כֻלָּם אֶת עוֹל
מַלְכוּתֶךָ, וְתִמְלוֹךְ עֲלֵיהֶם
מְהֵרָה לְעוֹלָם וָעֶד, כִּי
הַמַּלְכוּת שֶׁלְּךָ הִיא, וּלְעוֹלְמֵי עַד
תִּמְלוֹךְ בְּכָבוֹד, כַּכָּתוּב
בְּתוֹרָתֶךָ: יְיָ יִמְלֹךְ לְעֹלָם
וָעֶד. וְנֶאֱמַר: וְהָיָה יְיָ
לְמֶלֶךְ עַל כָּל הָאָרֶץ, בַּיּוֹם
הַהוּא יִהְיֶה יְיָ אֶחָד
וּשְׁמוֹ אֶחָד:

And therefore we hope to You, Lord our God, that we may speedily behold the splendor of Your might, to banish idolatry from the earth — and false gods will be utterly destroyed; to perfect the world under the sovereignty of the Almighty. All mankind shall invoke Your Name, to turn to You all the wicked of the earth. Then all the inhabitants of the world will recognize and know that every knee should bend to You, every tongue should swear [by Your Name]. Before You, Lord our God, they will bow and prostrate themselves, and give honor to the glory of Your Name; and they will all take upon themselves the

yoke of Your kingdom. May You soon reign over them forever and ever, for kingship is Yours, and to all eternity You will reign in glory, as it is written in Your Torah: The Lord will reign forever and ever. And it is said: The Lord shall be King over the entire earth; on that day the Lord shall be One and His Name One.

Mourner's Kaddish

קַדִּישׁ יָתוֹם

Recited standing, by mourners.

Yis-gadal v'yis-kadash °sh'may raböh°:	יִתְגַּדַּל וְיִתְקַדַּשׁ° שְׁמֵהּ רַבָּא°:
(Cong: Ömayn)	אמן
B'öl'mö di v'rö chir'u-say	בְּעָלְמָא דִּי בְרָא כִרְעוּתֵהּ
v'yamlich mal'chusay, v'yatzmach	וְיַמְלִיךְ מַלְכוּתֵהּ, וְיַצְמַח
purkönay °vikörayv m'shi-chay°.	פּוּרְקָנֵהּ °וִיקָרֵב מְשִׁיחֵהּ°:
(Cong: Ömayn)	אמן
B'cha-yay-chon uv'yomaychon.	בְּחַיֵּיכוֹן וּבְיוֹמֵיכוֹן
uv'chayay d'chöl bays yisrö-ayl,	וּבְחַיֵּי דְכָל בֵּית יִשְׂרָאֵל,
-agölö uviz'man köriv °v'im'ru ömayn°	בַּעֲגָלָא וּבִזְמַן קָרִיב °וְאִמְרוּ אָמֵן°:
(Cong.: Ömayn. °Y'hay sh'may rabö m'vörach	אמן °יְהֵא שְׁמֵהּ רַבָּא מְבָרַךְ
l'ölam ul'öl'may öl'ma-yöh Yisböraych°).	לְעָלַם וּלְעָלְמֵי עָלְמַיָּא יִתְבָּרַךְ°:
Yisböraych° °v'yishtabach, v'yispö-ayr,	יִתְבָּרַךְ° °וְיִשְׁתַּבַּח, וְיִתְפָּאַר,
v'yisromöm, v'yis-nasay, v'yis-hadör,	וְיִתְרוֹמָם, וְיִתְנַשֵּׂא, וְיִתְהַדָּר,
v'yis-aleh, v'yis-halöl°, °sh'may	וְיִתְעַלֶּה, וְיִתְהַלָּל°, °שְׁמֵהּ
d'kud-shö b'rich hu°.	דְּקֻדְשָׁא בְּרִיךְ הוּא°:
(Cong: Ömayn)	אמן

119

L'aylö min köl bir'chösö v'shirösö,	לְעֵלָּא מִן כָּל בִּרְכָתָא וְשִׁירָתָא,
tush-b'chösö v'ne-che-mösö,	תֻּשְׁבְּחָתָא וְנֶחֱמָתָא,
da-amirön b'öl'mö, °v'im'ru ömayn°.	דַּאֲמִירָן בְּעָלְמָא, °וְאִמְרוּ אָמֵן°:
(Cong: Ömayn)	אמן
Y'hay sh'lömö rabö min sh'ma-yö	יְהֵא שְׁלָמָא רַבָּא מִן שְׁמַיָּא
v'cha-yim tovim ölaynu v'al köl	וְחַיִּים טוֹבִים עָלֵינוּ וְעַל כָּל
yisrö-ayl °v'im'ru ömayn°.	יִשְׂרָאֵל °וְאִמְרוּ אָמֵן°:
(Cong: Ömayn)	אמן
>O-seh shölom (Between Rosh Hashana	>עֹשֶׂה שָׁלוֹם
and Yom Kippur substitute: ha-shölom)	(בעש״ת: הַשָּׁלוֹם)
bim'romöv, ^hu <ya-aseh shölom	בִּמְרוֹמָיו, ^הוּא >יַעֲשֶׂה
ölaynu ^v'al köl yisrö-ayl,	שָׁלוֹם עָלֵינוּ ^וְעַל כָּל יִשְׂרָאֵל,
°v'im'ru ömayn°. (Cong: Ömayn)	°וְאִמְרוּ אָמֵן°: אמן

(English translation of the Mourner's Kaddish can be found on page 71.)

Do Not Fear...   ...אַל תִּירָא

These meaningful verses express an important message to us as we conclude the service and are about to part ways. They remind us that no matter how long our exile may be, or what fears and anxieties beset us, God will always 'carry' us. We are God's 'burden' and responsibility, and God will never drop this burden. He will surely deliver us from our enemies and from the exile.

Al tirö mipachad pis-om,	אַל תִּירָא מִפַּחַד פִּתְאֹם,
umisho-as r'shö-im ki sövo.	וּמִשֹּׁאַת רְשָׁעִים כִּי תָבֹא:

Utzu ay-tzöh v'suför, dab'ru dövör	עֻצוּ עֵצָה וְתֻפָר, דַּבְּרוּ דָבָר
v'lo yökum, ki imönu ayl.	וְלֹא יָקוּם, כִּי עִמָּנוּ אֵל :
V'ad zik-nöh ani hu, v'ad sayvöh	וְעַד זִקְנָה אֲנִי הוּא, וְעַד שֵׂיבָה
ani esbol, ani ösisi va-ani	אֲנִי אֶסְבֹּל, אֲנִי עָשִׂיתִי וַאֲנִי
esö, va-ani esbol va-amalayt.	אֶשָּׂא, וַאֲנִי אֶסְבֹּל וַאֲמַלֵּט :
Ach tzadikim yodu lish'mechö	אַךְ צַדִּיקִים יוֹדוּ לִשְׁמֶךָ
yay-sh'vu y'shörim es pönechö.	יֵשְׁבוּ יְשָׁרִים אֶת פָּנֶיךָ :

Do not fear sudden terror, nor the destruction of the wicked when it comes. Contrive a scheme, but it will be foiled; conspire a plot but it will not materialize, for God is with us. To your old age I am [with you]; to your hoary years I will sustain you; I have made you, and I will carry you; I will sustain you and deliver you. Indeed, the righteous will extol Your Name; the upright will dwell in Your presence.

Kaddish D'Rabbonon   קַדִּישׁ דְּרַבָּנָן

Concluding *Mishnayot* before *Kaddish*. For the complete reading, see page 124.

Hitbil bo es ha-mitö, af al pi	הִטְבִּיל בּוֹ אֶת הַמִּטָּה, אַף עַל פִּי
she-raglehö shok'os ba-tit hö-öveh,	שֶׁרַגְלֶיהָ שׁוֹקְעוֹת בַּטִּיט הֶעָבֶה,
t'horöh, mip'nay shehama-yim	טְהוֹרָה, מִפְּנֵי שֶׁהַמַּיִם
m'kad'min. Mikveh shemay-möv	מְקַדְּמִין. מִקְוֶה שֶׁמֵּימָיו
m'rudödin, kovaysh afilu chavilay	מְרֻדָּדִין, כּוֹבֵשׁ אֲפִילוּ חֲבִילֵי

aytzim, afilu chavilay konim, k'day
she-yi-sp'chu ha-ma-yim, v'yorayd
v'tovayl. Machat shehi n'sunöh al
ma-alos ha-m'öröh, hö-yöh molich
umayvi bama-yim, kayvön she-övar
ölehö ha-gal, t'horöh.

עֵצִים, אֲפִילוּ חֲבִילֵי קָנִים, כְּדֵי
שֶׁיִּתְפְּחוּ הַמַּיִם, וְיוֹרֵד
וְטוֹבֵל. מַחַט שֶׁהִיא נְתוּנָה עַל
מַעֲלוֹת הַמְּעָרָה, הָיָה מוֹלִיךְ
וּמֵבִיא בַּמַּיִם, כֵּיוָן שֶׁעָבַר
עָלֶיהָ הַגַּל, טְהוֹרָה :

Rabi cha-nan-yö ben akash-yö omayr:
Rö-tzö ha-ködosh böruch hu l'zakos
es yirö-ayl, l'fichoch hirböh löhem
toröh umitzvos, shene-emar,
adonöy chöfaytz l'ma-an tzidko
yagdil toröh v'ya-dir.

רַבִּי חֲנַנְיָא בֶּן עֲקַשְׁיָא אוֹמֵר :
רָצָה הַקָּדוֹשׁ בָּרוּךְ הוּא לְזַכּוֹת
אֶת יִשְׂרָאֵל, לְפִיכָךְ הִרְבָּה לָהֶם
תּוֹרָה וּמִצְוֹת, שֶׁנֶּאֱמַר :
יְיָ חָפֵץ לְמַעַן צִדְקוֹ
יַגְדִּיל תּוֹרָה וְיַאְדִּיר :

If one immersed a bed [that is too tall to be immersed all at one time in a mikveh of forty se'ah], even if its legs sank into the thick mud, it nevertheless becomes ritually clean because the water touched them before [they sank into the mud]. A mikveh whose water is too shallow [for proper immersion], one may press down even bundles of sticks, even bundles of reeds, so that the level of the water is raised and then he may go down and immerse himself. A needle which is placed on the step [leading down to a mikveh] in a cave, and the water is moved back and forth, as soon as a wave has passed over it, it becomes ritually clean. Rabbi Chananyah ben Akashya said: The Holy One, blessed be He, wished to make the people of Israel meritorious; therefore He gave them Torah and mitzvot in abundant measure, as it is written: The Lord desired, for the sake of his [Israel's] righteousness, to make the Torah great and glorious.

Yis-gadal v'yis-kadash °sh'may raböh°:	יִתְגַּדַּל וְיִתְקַדַּשׁ ° שְׁמֵהּ רַבָּא °:
(Cong: Ömayn)	אמן
B'öl'mö di v'rö chir'u-say	בְּעָלְמָא דִּי בְרָא כִרְעוּתֵהּ
v'yamlich mal'chusay, v'yatzmach	וְיַמְלִיךְ מַלְכוּתֵהּ, וְיַצְמַח
purkönay °vikörayv m'shi-chay°:	פּוּרְקָנֵהּ ° וִיקָרֵב מְשִׁיחֵהּ °:
(Cong: Ömayn)	אמן
B'cha-yay-chon uv'yomaychon.	בְּחַיֵּיכוֹן וּבְיוֹמֵיכוֹן
uv'chayay d'chöl bays yisrö-ayl,	וּבְחַיֵּי דְכָל בֵּית יִשְׂרָאֵל,
-agölö uviz'man köriv °v'im'ru ömayn° :	בַּעֲגָלָא וּבִזְמַן קָרִיב ° וְאִמְרוּ אָמֵן °:
(Cong.: Ömayn. °Y'hay sh'may rabö m'vörach	אמן ° יְהֵא שְׁמֵהּ רַבָּא מְבָרַךְ
l'ölam ul'öl'may öl'ma-yöh Yisböraych°).	לְעָלַם וּלְעָלְמֵי עָלְמַיָּא יִתְבָּרַךְ°
Yisböraych° °v'yishtabach, v'yispö-ayr,	יִתְבָּרַךְ ° וְיִשְׁתַּבַּח, וְיִתְפָּאַר,
v'yisromöm, v'yis-nasay, v'yis-hadör,	וְיִתְרוֹמָם, וְיִתְנַשֵּׂא, וְיִתְהַדָּר,
v'yis-aleh, v'yis-halöl°, °sh'may	וְיִתְעַלֶּה, וְיִתְהַלָּל °, שְׁמֵהּ°
d'kud-shö b'rich hu°.	דְּקֻדְשָׁא בְּרִיךְ הוּא °:
(Cong: Ömayn)	אמן
L'aylö min köl bir'chösö v'shirösö,	לְעֵלָּא מִן כָּל בִּרְכָתָא וְשִׁירָתָא,
tush-b'chösö v'ne-che-mösö,	תֻּשְׁבְּחָתָא וְנֶחֱמָתָא,
da-amirön b'öl'mö, °v'im'ru ömayn°.	דַּאֲמִירָן בְּעָלְמָא, ° וְאִמְרוּ אָמֵן °:
(Cong: Ömayn)	אמן
Al yisrö-ayl v'al rabönön, v'al	עַל יִשְׂרָאֵל וְעַל רַבָּנָן, וְעַל
tal-midayhon, v'al köl tal-miday	תַּלְמִידֵיהוֹן וְעַל כָּל תַּלְמִידֵי
sal-midayhon, v'al köl mön d'ös'kin	תַלְמִידֵיהוֹן, וְעַל כָּל מָאן דְּעָסְקִין
b'oray'sö, di v'asrö hödayn, v'di	בְּאוֹרַיְתָא, דִּי בְאַתְרָא הָדֵין וְדִי

123

v'chöl asar v'asar, y'hay l'hon ul'chon
sh'lömö rabö, chinö v'chisdö
v'rachamin v'cha-yin arichin,
um'zonö r'vichö ufur'könö, min
ködöm avu-hon d'vish'ma-yö
v'im'ru ömayn.

בְּכָל אֲתַר וַאֲתַר, יְהֵא לְהוֹן וּלְכוֹן
שְׁלָמָא רַבָּא חִנָּא וְחִסְדָּא
וְרַחֲמִין וְחַיִּין אֲרִיכִין,
וּמְזוֹנָא רְוִיחָא וּפוּרְקָנָא, מִן
קֳדָם אֲבוּהוֹן דְּבִשְׁמַיָּא
וְאִמְרוּ אָמֵן :

(Cong: Ömayn)
אמן

Y'hay sh'lömö rabö min sh'ma-yö,
v'cha-yim tovim ölaynu v'al köl
yisrö-ayl °v'im'ru ömayn°.

יְהֵא שְׁלָמָא רַבָּא מִן שְׁמַיָּא
וְחַיִּים טוֹבִים עָלֵינוּ וְעַל כָּל
יִשְׂרָאֵל וְאִמְרוּ אָמֵן°

(Cong: Ömayn)
אמן

>O-seh shölom (Between Rosh Hashana
and Yom Kippur substitute: ha-shölom)
bim'romöv, ^hu <ya-aseh shölom
ölaynu ^v'al köl yisrö-ayl,
°v'im'ru ömayn°. (Cong: Ömayn)

<עֹשֶׂה שָׁלוֹם
(בעשי״ת: הַשָּׁלוֹם)
בִּמְרוֹמָיו,^ הוּא <יַעֲשֶׂה
שָׁלוֹם עָלֵינוּ ^וְעַל כָּל יִשְׂרָאֵל,
וְאִמְרוּ אָמֵן° : אמן

Mishnayot Learning for a Mourner

Throughout the twelve months following the passing of one's father or mother, and on the anniversary of their passing (known as the Yahrzeit), it is appropriate to learn *Mishnayot* of the order *Taharot*, especially the following two chapters.

כלים פרק כד

(א) שְׁלֹשָׁה תְרִיסִין הֵם, תְּרִיס הַכָּפוּף, טָמֵא מִדְרָס, וְשֶׁמְּשַׂחֲקִין בּוֹ בַּקֻּנְפּוֹן, טָמֵא טְמֵא מֵת, וְדִיצַת הָעַרְבִיִּין טְהוֹרָה מִכְּלוּם : (ב) שָׁלֹשׁ עֲגָלוֹת הֵן, הָעֲשׂוּיָה כְּקַתֶּדְרָא, טְמֵאָה מִדְרָס, כְּמִטָּה, טְמֵאָה טְמֵא מֵת. וְשֶׁל אֲבָנִים, טְהוֹרָה מִכְּלוּם : (ג) שָׁלֹשׁ עֲרֵבוֹת הֵן, עֲרֵבָה מִשְּׁנֵי לוּגִּין עַד תִּשְׁעָה קַבִּין שֶׁנִּסְדְּקָה, טְמֵאָה מִדְרָס, שְׁלֵמָה, טְמֵאָה טְמֵא מֵת. וְהַבָּאָה בַּמִּדָּה, טְהוֹרָה מִכְּלוּם :

(ד) שָׁלֹשׁ תֵּבוֹת הֵן, תֵּבָה שֶׁפִּתְחָהּ מִצִּדָּהּ, טְמֵאָה מִדְרָס, מִלְמַעְלָן, טְמֵאָה טְמֵא מֵת. וְהַבָּאָה בַמִּדָּה, טְהוֹרָה מִכְּלוּם: (ה) שְׁלֹשָׁה תַרְבּוֹסִין הֵן, שֶׁל סַפָּרִין, טָמֵא מִדְרָס, שֶׁאוֹכְלִין עָלָיו, טָמֵא טְמֵא מֵת. וְשֶׁל זֵיתִים, טָהוֹר מִכְּלוּם: (ו) שָׁלֹשׁ בְּסִיסִיּוֹת הֵן, שֶׁלִּפְנֵי הַמִּטָּה וְשֶׁלִּפְנֵי סוֹפְרִים, טְמֵאָה מִדְרָס, וְשֶׁל דְּלַפְקִי, טְמֵאָה טְמֵא מֵת, וְשֶׁל מִגְדָּל, טְהוֹרָה מִכְּלוּם: (ז) שָׁלֹשׁ פִּנְקָסִיּוֹת הֵן, הָאַפִּיפוֹרִין, טְמֵאָה מִדְרָס, וְשֶׁיֵּשׁ בָּהּ בֵּית קִבּוּל שַׁעֲוָה, טְמֵאָה טְמֵא מֵת, וַחֲלָקָה, טְהוֹרָה מִכְּלוּם: (ח) שָׁלֹשׁ מִטּוֹת הֵן, הָעֲשׂוּיָה לִשְׁכִיבָה, טְמֵאָה מִדְרָס, שֶׁל זַגָּגִין, טְמֵאָה טְמֵא מֵת, וְשֶׁל סָרָגִין, טְהוֹרָה מִכְּלוּם: (ט) שָׁלֹשׁ מַשְׁפֵּלוֹת הֵן, שֶׁל זֶבֶל, טְמֵאָה מִדְרָס, שֶׁל תֶּבֶן, טְמֵאָה טְמֵא מֵת, וְהַפּוּחְלָץ שֶׁל גְּמַלִּים, טָהוֹר מִכְּלוּם: (י) שָׁלֹשׁ מַפּוֹצִים הֵן, הָעֲשׂוּיָה לִישִׁיבָה, טְמֵאָה מִדְרָס, שֶׁל צַבָּעִין, טָמֵא טְמֵא מֵת, וְשֶׁל גִּתּוֹת, טָהוֹר מִכְּלוּם: (יא) שָׁלֹשׁ חֲמָתוֹת, וְשָׁלֹשׁ תּוּרְמָלִין הֵן, הַמְקַבְּלִין כַּשִּׁעוּר, טְמֵאִין מִדְרָס, וְשֶׁאֵינָן מְקַבְּלִין כַּשִּׁעוּר, טְמֵאִין טְמֵא מֵת, וְשֶׁל עוֹר הַדָּג, טָהוֹר מִכְּלוּם: (יב) שְׁלֹשָׁה עוֹרוֹת הֵן, הֶעָשׂוּי לְשָׁטִיחַ, טָמֵא מִדְרָס, לְתַכְרִיךְ הַכֵּלִים, טָמֵא טְמֵא מֵת, וְשֶׁל רְצוּעוֹת וְשֶׁל סַנְדָּלִים, טְהוֹרָה מִכְּלוּם: (יג) שְׁלֹשָׁה סְדִינִין הֵן, הֶעָשׂוּי לִשְׁכִיבָה, טָמֵא מִדְרָס, לְוִילוֹן, טָמֵא טְמֵא מֵת, וְשֶׁל צוּרוֹת, טָהוֹר מִכְּלוּם: (יד) שָׁלֹשׁ מִטְפָּחוֹת הֵן, שֶׁל יָדַיִם, טְמֵאָה מִדְרָס, שֶׁל סְפָרִין, טְמֵאָה טְמֵא מֵת, וְשֶׁל תַּכְרִיךְ (וְשֶׁל) נִבְלֵי בְנֵי לֵוִי, טְהוֹרָה מִכְּלוּם: (טו) שְׁלֹשָׁה פְּרַקְלִינִין הֵן, שֶׁל צָדֵי חַיָּה וָעוֹף, טָמֵא מִדְרָס, שֶׁל חֲגָבִין, טָמֵא טְמֵא מֵת, וְשֶׁל קַיָּצִין, טָהוֹר מִכְּלוּם: (טז) שָׁלֹשׁ סְבָכוֹת הֵן, שֶׁל יַלְדָּה, טְמֵאָה מִדְרָס, שֶׁל זְקֵנָה, טְמֵאָה טְמֵא מֵת, וְשֶׁל יוֹצֵאת לַחוּץ, טְהוֹרָה מִכְּלוּם: (יז) שָׁלֹשׁ קֻפּוֹת הֵן, מְהוּהָה שֶׁטְּלָיָהּ עַל הַבְּרִיָּה, הוֹלְכִין אַחַר הַבְּרִיָּה, קְטַנָּה עַל הַגְּדוֹלָה, הוֹלְכִין אַחַר הַגְּדוֹלָה, הָיוּ שָׁווֹת, הוֹלְכִין אַחַר הַפְּנִימִית, רַבִּי שִׁמְעוֹן אוֹמֵר, כַּף מֹאזְנַיִם שֶׁטְּלָיָהּ עַל שׁוּלֵי הַמֵּיחַם, מִבִּפְנִים טָמֵא, מִבַּחוּץ טָהוֹר. טְלָיָהּ עַל צִדָּהּ, בֵּין מִבִּפְנִים בֵּין מִבַּחוּץ, טָהוֹר:

מקואות פרק ז

(א) יֵשׁ מַעֲלִין אֶת הַמִּקְוֶה וְלֹא פוֹסְלִין, פּוֹסְלִין וְלֹא מַעֲלִין, לֹא מַעֲלִין וְלֹא פוֹסְלִין, אֵלּוּ מַעֲלִין וְלֹא פוֹסְלִין, הַשֶּׁלֶג, וְהַבָּרָד, וְהַכְּפוֹר, וְהַגְּלִיד, וְהַמֶּלַח, וְהַטִּיט הַנָּרוֹק, אָמַר רַבִּי עֲקִיבָא, הָיָה רַבִּי יִשְׁמָעֵאל דָּן כְּנֶגְדִּי לוֹמַר, הַשֶּׁלֶג אֵינוֹ מַעֲלֶה אֶת הַמִּקְוֶה, וְהֵעִידוּ אַנְשֵׁי מֵידְבָא מִשְּׁמוֹ, שֶׁאָמַר לָהֶם צְאוּ וְהָבִיאוּ שֶׁלֶג וַעֲשׂוּ מִקְוֶה בַּתְּחִלָּה, רַבִּי יוֹחָנָן בֶּן נוּרִי אוֹמֵר, אֶבֶן הַבָּרָד כַּמָּיִם. כֵּיצַד מַעֲלִין וְלֹא פוֹסְלִין, מִקְוֶה שֶׁיֶּשׁ בּוֹ אַרְבָּעִים סְאָה חָסֵר אַחַת, נָפַל מֵהֶם סְאָה לְתוֹכוֹ וְהֶעֱלָהוּ, נִמְצְאוּ מַעֲלִין וְלֹא פוֹסְלִין: (ב) אֵלּוּ פוֹסְלִין וְלֹא מַעֲלִין, הַמַּיִם בֵּין טְמֵאִים בֵּין

טְהוֹרִים, וּמֵי כְבָשִׁים וּמֵי שְׁלָקוֹת, וְהַתֶּמֶד עַד שֶׁלֹּא הֶחְמִיץ. כֵּיצַד פּוֹסְלִין וְלֹא מַעֲלִין, מִקְוֶה שֶׁיֵּשׁ בּוֹ אַרְבָּעִים סְאָה חָסֵר קְרְטוֹב וְנָפַל מֵהֶן קְרְטוֹב לְתוֹכוֹ, לֹא הֶעֱלָהוּ, וּפוֹסְלוֹ בִּשְׁלֹשָׁה לֻגִּין, אֲבָל שְׁאָר הַמַּשְׁקִין, וּמֵי פֵרוֹת, וְהַצִּיר, וְהַמֻּרְיָס, וְהַתֶּמֶד מִשֶּׁהֶחְמִיץ, פְּעָמִים מַעֲלִין וּפְעָמִים שֶׁאֵינָן מַעֲלִין, כֵּיצַד, מִקְוֶה שֶׁיֵּשׁ בּוֹ אַרְבָּעִים סְאָה חָסֵר אַחַת, נָפַל לְתוֹכוֹ סְאָה מֵהֶם, לֹא הֶעֱלָהוּ, הָיוּ בוֹ אַרְבָּעִים סְאָה, נָתַן סְאָה וְנָטַל סְאָה, הֲרֵי זֶה כָשֵׁר: (ג) הֵדִיחַ בּוֹ סַלֵּי זֵיתִים וְסַלֵּי עֲנָבִים, וְשִׁנּוּ אֶת מַרְאָיו, כָּשֵׁר, רַבִּי יוֹסֵי אוֹמֵר, מֵי הַצֶּבַע פּוֹסְלִין אוֹתוֹ בִּשְׁלֹשָׁה לֻגִּין, וְאֵינָן פּוֹסְלִין אוֹתוֹ בְּשִׁנּוּי מַרְאֶה, נָפַל לְתוֹכוֹ יַיִן וּמֹחַל, וְשִׁנּוּ אֶת מַרְאָיו, פָּסוּל, כֵּיצַד יַעֲשֶׂה, יַמְתִּין לוֹ עַד שֶׁיֵּרְדוּ גְשָׁמִים וְיַחְזְרוּ מַרְאֵיהֶן לְמַרְאֵה הַמַּיִם, הָיוּ בוֹ אַרְבָּעִים סְאָה, מִלֵּא בַכָּתֵף, וְנוֹתֵן לְתוֹכוֹ עַד שֶׁיַּחְזְרוּ מַרְאֵיהֶן לְמַרְאֵה הַמָּיִם: (ד) נָפַל לְתוֹכוֹ יַיִן, אוֹ מֹחַל וְשִׁנּוּ מִקְצָת מַרְאָיו, אִם אֵין בּוֹ מַרְאֵה מַיִם אַרְבָּעִים סְאָה, הֲרֵי זֶה לֹא יִטְבֹּל בּוֹ: (ה) שְׁלֹשָׁה לֻגִּין מַיִם, וְנָפַל לְתוֹכָן קְרְטוֹב יַיִן, וַהֲרֵי מַרְאֵיהֶן כְּמַרְאֵה הַיַּיִן, וְנָפְלוּ לַמִּקְוֶה, לֹא פְסָלוּהוּ, שְׁלֹשָׁה לֻגִּין מַיִם חָסֵר קְרְטוֹב, וְנָפַל לְתוֹכָן קְרְטוֹב חָלָב, וַהֲרֵי מַרְאֵיהֶן כְּמַרְאֵה הַמַּיִם, וְנָפְלוּ לַמִּקְוֶה, לֹא פְסָלוּהוּ. רַבִּי יוֹחָנָן בֶּן נוּרִי אוֹמֵר, הַכֹּל הוֹלֵךְ אַחַר הַמַּרְאֶה: (ו) מִקְוֶה שֶׁיֵּשׁ בּוֹ אַרְבָּעִים סְאָה מְכֻוָּנוֹת, יָרְדוּ שְׁנַיִם וְטָבְלוּ זֶה אַחַר זֶה, הָרִאשׁוֹן טָהוֹר, וְהַשֵּׁנִי טָמֵא. רַבִּי יְהוּדָה אוֹמֵר, אִם הָיוּ רַגְלָיו שֶׁל רִאשׁוֹן נוֹגְעוֹת בַּמַּיִם, אַף הַשֵּׁנִי טָהוֹר, הִטְבִּיל בּוֹ אֶת הַסָּגוֹס וְהֶעֱלָהוּ, מִקְצָתוֹ נוֹגֵעַ בַּמַּיִם, טָהוֹר, הַכַּר וְהַכֶּסֶת שֶׁל עוֹר, כֵּיוָן שֶׁהִגְבִּיהַּ שְׂפְתוֹתֵיהֶם מִן הַמַּיִם, הַמַּיִם שֶׁבְּתוֹכָן שְׁאוּבִין, כֵּיצַד יַעֲשֶׂה, מַטְבִּילָן וּמַעֲלֶה אוֹתָם דֶּרֶךְ שׁוּלֵיהֶם.

The Counting of the Omer

The Omer is counted near the end of the evening services from the second night of Passover until the night before Shavuot. If one forgot to count the Omer at night he should count it during the day without a blessing. If, however, he had forgotten to count also during the entire day, he must count every night thereafter without reciting the blessing.

Recited Standing

Böruch atöh adonöy elohaynu, בָּרוּךְ אַתָּה יְיָ אֱלֹהֵינוּ,

melech hö-olöm, asher kid'shönu מֶלֶךְ הָעוֹלָם, אֲשֶׁר קִדְּשָׁנוּ

b'mitzvosöv, v'tzivönu al בְּמִצְוֹתָיו, וְצִוָּנוּ עַל

s'firas hö-omer. סְפִירַת הָעֹמֶר.

Blessed are You, Lord our God, King of the Universe, who has sanctified us with His commandments, and commanded us concerning the counting of the Omer.

Ha-yom yom echöd lö-omer. הַיּוֹם יוֹם אֶחָד לָעֹמֶר:

(Chesed she-b'chesed) חסד שבחסד

Today is the first day of the Omer.

Continue below. On all other days count the Omer as listed on pages 131-135.

Höracha-mön hu ya-chazir lönu הָרַחֲמָן הוּא יַחֲזִיר לָנוּ

avodas bays ha-mikdösh lim'komöh, עֲבוֹדַת בֵּית הַמִּקְדָּשׁ לִמְקוֹמָהּ,

bim'hayröh v'yömaynu ömayn selöh. בִּמְהֵרָה בְיָמֵינוּ אָמֵן סֶלָה.

May the Merciful One restore unto us the service of the Beit Hamikdosh (Holy Temple) to its place, speedily in our days; Amen, Selah.

127

Lam'natzay-ach bin'ginos
mizmor shir. Elohim y'chö-naynu
vivö-r'chauny, yö-ayr pönöv itönu,
selöh. Löda-as bö-öretz darkechö,
b'chöl goyim y'shu-ösechö. Yoduchö
amim elohim, yoduchö amim kulöm.
Yis-m'chu viran'nu l'umim, ki sishpot
amim mishor, ul'umim bö-öretz
tan-chaym selöh. Yoduchö amim
elohim, yoduchö amim kulöm. Eretz
nös'nöh y'vulöh, y'vör'chaynu elohim
elohaynu. Y'vör'chaynu elohim,
v'y-ir'u oso köl af'sei öretz.

לַמְנַצֵּחַ בִּנְגִינֹת
מִזְמוֹר שִׁיר: אֱלֹהִים יְחָנֵּנוּ
וִיבָרְכֵנוּ, יָאֵר פָּנָיו אִתָּנוּ,
סֶלָה: לָדַעַת בָּאָרֶץ דַּרְכֶּךָ,
בְּכָל גּוֹיִם יְשׁוּעָתֶךָ: יוֹדוּךָ
עַמִּים אֱלֹהִים, יוֹדוּךָ עַמִּים כֻּלָּם:
יִשְׂמְחוּ וִירַנְּנוּ לְאֻמִּים, כִּי תִשְׁפֹּט
עַמִּים מִישֹׁר, וּלְאֻמִּים בָּאָרֶץ
תַּנְחֵם סֶלָה: יוֹדוּךָ עַמִּים
אֱלֹהִים, יוֹדוּךָ עַמִּים כֻּלָּם: אֶרֶץ
נָתְנָה יְבוּלָהּ, יְבָרְכֵנוּ אֱלֹהִים
אֱלֹהֵינוּ: יְבָרְכֵנוּ אֱלֹהִים,
וְיִירְאוּ אוֹתוֹ כָּל אַפְסֵי אָרֶץ:

For the Choirmaster; a song with instrumental music; a Psalm. May God be gracious to us and bless us, may He make His countenance shine upon us forever; that Your way be known on earth, Your salvation among all nations. The nations will extol You, O God; all the nations will extol You. The nations will rejoice and sing for joy, for You will judge the peoples justly and guide the nations on earth forever. The peoples will extol You, O God; all the peoples will extol You, for the earth will have yielded its produce and God, our God, will bless us. God will bless us; and all, from the farthest corners of the earth, shall fear Him.

Önö, b'cho-ach g'dulas y'min'chö,
tatir tz'ruröh. Kabayl rinas am'chö,

אָנָּא, בְּכֹחַ גְּדֻלַּת יְמִינְךָ,
תַּתִּיר צְרוּרָה: קַבֵּל רִנַּת עַמְּךָ,

128

sag'vaynu, taha-raynu, noröh.	שַׂגְּבֵנוּ, טַהֲרֵנוּ, נוֹרָא :
Nö gibor, dor'shay yichud'chö,	נָא גִבּוֹר, דּוֹרְשֵׁי יִחוּדְךָ,
k'vövas shöm'raym. Bö-r'chaym	כְּבָבַת שָׁמְרֵם : בָּרְכֵם
taha-raym, rachamay tzid'kös'chö	טַהֲרֵם, רַחֲמֵי צִדְקָתְךָ
tömid göm'laym. Chasin ködosh,	תָּמִיד גָּמְלֵם : חֲסִין קָדוֹשׁ,
b'rov tuv'chö nahayl adösechö.	בְּרוֹב טוּבְךָ נַהֵל עֲדָתֶךָ :
Yöchid, gay-eh, l'am'chö p'nay,	יָחִיד, גֵּאֶה, לְעַמְּךָ פְּנֵה,
zoch'ray k'dushösechö. Shav-ösaynu	זוֹכְרֵי קְדֻשָּׁתֶךָ : שַׁוְעָתֵנוּ
kabayl, ush'ma tza-akösaynu,	קַבֵּל, וּשְׁמַע צַעֲקָתֵנוּ,
yoday-a ta-alumos. Böruch shaym	יוֹדֵעַ תַּעֲלוּמוֹת : בָּרוּךְ שֵׁם
k'vod mal'chuso l'olöm vö-ed.	כְּבוֹד מַלְכוּתוֹ לְעוֹלָם וָעֶד :

We implore you, by the great power of Your right hand, release the captive. Accept the prayer of Your people; strengthen us, purify us, Awesome One. Mighty One, we beseech You, guard as the apple of the eye those who seek Your Oneness. Bless them, cleanse them; bestow upon them forever Your merciful righteousness. Powerful, Holy One, in Your abounding goodness, guide Your congregation. Only and Exalted One, turn to Your people who are mindful of Your holiness. Accept our supplication and hear our cry, You who know secret thoughts. Blessed be the name of the glory of His kingdom forever and ever.

Ribono shel olöm, atöh tzivisönu	רִבּוֹנוֹ שֶׁל עוֹלָם, אַתָּה צִוִּיתָנוּ
al y'day mosheh avdechö lispor	עַל יְדֵי מֹשֶׁה עַבְדֶּךָ לִסְפּוֹר
s'firas hö-omer k'day l'taharaynu	סְפִירַת הָעוֹמֶר כְּדֵי לְטַהֲרֵנוּ
mik'lipo-saynu umitum-osaynu,	מִקְּלִפּוֹתֵינוּ וּמִטֻּמְאוֹתֵינוּ,

129

k'mo she-kösavtö b'sorösechö:	כְּמוֹ שֶׁכָּתַבְתָּ בְּתוֹרָתֶךְ:
Us'fartem löchem mi-möchöras	וּסְפַרְתֶּם לָכֶם מִמָּחֳרַת
ha-shabös mi-yom ha-vi-achem es	הַשַּׁבָּת מִיּוֹם הֲבִיאֲכֶם אֶת
omer ha-t'nuföh sheva shabösos	עֹמֶר הַתְּנוּפָה שֶׁבַע שַׁבָּתוֹת
t'mimos tih-yenöh, ad mi-möchöras	תְּמִימֹת תִּהְיֶינָה, עַד מִמָּחֳרַת
ha-shabös hash'vi-is tisp'ru chamishim	הַשַּׁבָּת הַשְּׁבִיעִת תִּסְפְּרוּ חֲמִשִּׁים
yom, k'day sheyitö-haru naf'shos	יוֹם, כְּדֵי שֶׁיִּטַּהֲרוּ נַפְשׁוֹת
am'chö yisrö-ayl mizuha-mösöm,	עַמְּךָ יִשְׂרָאֵל מִזֻּהֲמָתָם,
uv'chayn y'hi rötzon mil'fönechö,	וּבְכֵן יְהִי רָצוֹן מִלְּפָנֶיךָ,
adonöy elohaynu vay-lohay	יְיָ אֱלֹהֵינוּ וֵאלֹהֵי
avosaynu, shebiz'chus s'firas	אֲבוֹתֵינוּ, שֶׁבִּזְכוּת סְפִירַת
hö-omer shesö-farti ha-yom, y'sukan	הָעוֹמֶר שֶׁסָּפַרְתִּי הַיּוֹם, יְתֻקַּן
mah she-pögamti bis'firöh	מַה שֶּׁפָּגַמְתִּי בִּסְפִירָה
(say the appropiate Sefira)	(say the appropiate Sefira)
v'etöhayr v'eskadaysh bik'dushöh	וְאֶטָּהֵר וְאֶתְקַדֵּשׁ בִּקְדֻשָּׁה
shel ma-löh, v'al y'day zeh yushpa	שֶׁל מַעֲלָה, וְעַל יְדֵי זֶה יֻשְׁפַּע
shefa rav b'chöl hö-lömos	שֶׁפַע רַב בְּכָל הָעוֹלָמוֹת
ul'sakayn es naf'shosaynu	וּלְתַקֵּן אֶת נַפְשׁוֹתֵינוּ
v'ruchosaynu v'nish'mosaynu	וְרוּחוֹתֵינוּ וְנִשְׁמוֹתֵינוּ
miköl sig uf'gam ul'taharaynu	מִכָּל סִיג וּפְגַם וּלְטַהֲרֵנוּ
ul'kad'shaynu bik'dushös'cho	וּלְקַדְּשֵׁנוּ בִּקְדֻשָּׁתְךָ
hö-elyonöh, ömayn selöh.	הָעֶלְיוֹנָה, אָמֵן סֶלָה:

Master of the universe, You have commanded us through Moses Your servant to count Sefiras HaOmer, in order to purify us from our evil and uncleanness.

As You have written in Your Torah, "You shall count for yourselves from the day following the day of rest, from the day on which you bring the Omer as a wave-offering; [the counting] shall be for seven full weeks. Until the day following the seventh week shall you count fifty days," so that the souls of Your people Israel may be cleansed from their defilement. Therefore, may it be Your will, Lord our God and God of our fathers, that in the merit of the Sefiras HaOmer which I counted today, the blemish that I have caused in the sefirah (Specify the appropriate sefirah) *be rectified and I may be purified and sanctified with supernal holiness. May abundant bounty thereby be bestowed upon all the worlds. May it rectify our nefesh, ruach and neshamah from every baseness and defect, and may it purify and sanctify us with Your supernal holiness. Amen, selah.*

Continue with *Olaynu* (It is incumbent...), on page 116.

The Days of the Omer

The day of the Omer is counted as listed below. The *sefira* (to be inserted in the last paragraph) is writtren in parentheses.

Day 2: Ha-yom sh'nay yomim lö-omer.
(G'vurö Sheb'chesed)

2 - הַיּוֹם שְׁנֵי יָמִים לָעֹמֶר.
גבורה שבחסד

Day 3: Ha-yom sh'loshöh yömim lö-omer.
(Tif-eres Sheb'chesed)

3 - הַיּוֹם שְׁלֹשָׁה יָמִים לָעֹמֶר.
תפארת שבחסד

Day 4: Ha-yom arbö-öh yömim lö-omer.
(Ne-tzach Sheb'chesed)

4 - הַיּוֹם אַרְבָּעָה יָמִים לָעֹמֶר.
נצח שבחסד

Day 5: Ha-yom chamishöh yömim lö-omer.
(Hod Sheb'chesed)

5 - הַיּוֹם חֲמִשָּׁה יָמִים לָעֹמֶר.
הוד שבחסד

Day 6: Ha-yom shishöh yömim lö-omer.
(Y'sod Sheb'chesed)

6 - הַיּוֹם שִׁשָּׁה יָמִים לָעֹמֶר.
יסוד שבחסד

Day 7: Ha-yom shiv-öh yömim she-haym
shövu-a echöd lö-omer.
(Mal'chus Sheb'chesed)

7- הַיּוֹם שִׁבְעָה יָמִים שֶׁהֵם
שָׁבוּעַ אֶחָד לָעֹמֶר.
מלכות שבחסד

Day 8: Ha-yom sh'monöh yömim she-haym
shövu-a echöd v'yom echöd lö-omer.
(Chesed Shebig'vuröh)

8- הַיּוֹם שְׁמוֹנָה יָמִים שֶׁהֵם
שָׁבוּעַ אֶחָד וְיוֹם אֶחָד לָעֹמֶר.
חסד שבגבורה

Day 9: Ha-yom tish-öh yömim she-haym
shövu-a echöd ush'nay yömim lö-omer.
(G'vuröh Shebig'vuröh)

9- הַיּוֹם תִּשְׁעָה יָמִים שֶׁהֵם
שָׁבוּעַ אֶחָד וּשְׁנֵי יָמִים לָעֹמֶר.
גבורה שבגבורה

Day 10: Hayom asörö yömim she-haym
shövu-a echöd ush'loshöh yömim lö-omer.
(Tif-eres Shebig'vuröh)

10- הַיּוֹם עֲשָׂרָה יָמִים שֶׁהֵם
שָׁבוּעַ אֶחָד וּשְׁלֹשָׁה יָמִים לָעֹמֶר.
תפארת שבגבורה

Day 11: Ha-yom achad ösör yom she-haym
shövu-a echöd v'arbö-öh yömim lö-omer.
(Ne-tzach Shebig'vuröh)

11- הַיּוֹם אַחַד עָשָׂר יוֹם שֶׁהֵם
שָׁבוּעַ אֶחָד וְאַרְבָּעָה יָמִים לָעֹמֶר.
נצח שבגבורה

Day 12: Ha-yom sh'naym ösör yom she-haym
shövu-a echöd vacha-mishöh yömim lö-omer.
(Hod Shebig'vuröh)

12- הַיּוֹם שְׁנֵים עָשָׂר יוֹם שֶׁהֵם
שָׁבוּעַ אֶחָד וַחֲמִשָּׁה יָמִים לָעֹמֶר.
הוד שבגבורה

Day 13: Ha-yom shloshö ösör yom she-haym
shövu-a echöd v'shishö yömim lö-omer.
(Y'sod Shebig'vuröh)

13- הַיּוֹם שְׁלֹשָׁה עָשָׂר יוֹם שֶׁהֵם
שָׁבוּעַ אֶחָד וְשִׁשָּׁה יָמִים לָעֹמֶר.
יסוד שבגבורה

Day 14: Ha-yom arbö-öh ösör yom she-haym
sh'nay shövu-os lö-omer.
(Mal'chus Shebig'vuröh)

14- הַיּוֹם אַרְבָּעָה עָשָׂר יוֹם שֶׁהֵם
שְׁנֵי שָׁבוּעוֹת לָעֹמֶר.
מלכות שבגבורה

Day 15: Ha-yom chamishöh ösör yom she-haym
sh'nay shövu-os v'yom echöd lö-omer.
(Chesed Sheb'sif-eres)

15- הַיּוֹם חֲמִשָּׁה עָשָׂר יוֹם שֶׁהֵם
שְׁנֵי שָׁבוּעוֹת וְיוֹם אֶחָד לָעֹמֶר.
חסד שבתפארת

Day 16: Ha-yom shishö ösör yom she-haym
sh'nay shövu-os ush'nay yömim lö-omer.
(G'vuröh Sheb'sif-eres)

16- הַיּוֹם שִׁשָּׁה עָשָׂר יוֹם שֶׁהֵם
שְׁנֵי שָׁבוּעוֹת וּשְׁנֵי יָמִים לָעֹמֶר.
גבורה שבתפארת

Day 17: Ha-yom shiv-öh ösör yom she-haym
sh'nay shövu-os ush'loshöh yömim lö-omer.
(Tif-eres Sheb'sif-eres)

17- הַיּוֹם שִׁבְעָה עָשָׂר יוֹם שֶׁהֵם
שְׁנֵי שָׁבוּעוֹת וּשְׁלֹשָׁה יָמִים לָעֹמֶר.
תפארת שבתפארת

Day 18: Ha-yom sh'monöh ösör yom she-haym
sh'nay shövu-os v'arbö-öh yömimn lö-omer.
(Ne-tzach Sheb'sif-eres)

Day 19: Ha-yom tish-öh ösör yom she-haym
sh'nay shövu-os vacha-mishöh yömim lö-omer.
(Hod Sheb'sif-eres)

Day 20: Ha-yom esrim yom she-haym
sh'nay shövu-os v'shishöh yömim lö-omer.
(Y'sod Sheb'sif-eres)

Day 21: Ha-yom echöd v'esrim yom she-haym
sh'loshöh shövu-os lö-omer.
(Mal'chus Sheb'sif-eres)

Day 22: Ha-yom sh'na-yim v'esrim yom she-haym
sh'loshöh shövu-os v'yom echöd lö-omer.
(Chesed Sheb'netzach)

Day 23: Ha-yom sh'loshö v'esrim yom she-haym
sh'loshöh shövu-os ush'nay yömim lö-omer.
(G'vuröh Sheb'netzach)

Day 24: Ha-yom arbö-öh v'esrim yom she-haym
sh'loshöh shövu-os ush'loshö yömim lö-omer.
(Tif-'eres Sheb'ne-tzach)

Day 25: Ha-yom chamishöh v'esrim yom she-haym
sh'loshöh shövu-os v'arbö-öh yömim lö-omer.
(Ne-tzach Sheb'ne-tzach)

Day 26: Ha-yom shishöh v'esrim yom she-haym
sh'loshöh shövu-os vacha-mishöh yömim lö-omer.
(Hod Sheb'ne-tzach)

Day 27: Ha-yom shiv-öh v'esrim yom she-haym
sh'loshöh shövu-os v'shishöh yömim lö-omer.
(Y'sod Sheb'ne-tzach)

Day 28: Ha-yom sh'monöh v'esrim yom she-haym
arbö-öh shövu-os lö-omer.
(Mal'chus Sheb'ne-tzach)

18 - הַיּוֹם שְׁמוֹנָה עָשָׂר יוֹם שֶׁהֵם
שְׁנֵי שָׁבוּעוֹת וְאַרְבָּעָה יָמִים לָעֹמֶר.
נצח שבתפארת

19 - הַיּוֹם תִּשְׁעָה עָשָׂר יוֹם שֶׁהֵם
שְׁנֵי שָׁבוּעוֹת וַחֲמִשָּׁה יָמִים לָעֹמֶר.
הוד שבתפארת

20 - הַיּוֹם עֶשְׂרִים יוֹם שֶׁהֵם
שְׁנֵי שָׁבוּעוֹת וְשִׁשָּׁה יָמִים לָעֹמֶר.
יסוד שבתפארת

21 - הַיּוֹם אֶחָד וְעֶשְׂרִים יוֹם שֶׁהֵם
שְׁלֹשָׁה שָׁבוּעוֹת לָעֹמֶר.
מלכות שבתפארת

22 - הַיּוֹם שְׁנַיִם וְעֶשְׂרִים יוֹם שֶׁהֵם
שְׁלֹשָׁה שָׁבוּעוֹת וְיוֹם אֶחָד לָעֹמֶר.
חסד שבנצח

23 - הַיּוֹם שְׁלֹשָׁה וְעֶשְׂרִים יוֹם שֶׁהֵם
שְׁלֹשָׁה שָׁבוּעוֹת וּשְׁנֵי יָמִים לָעֹמֶר.
גבורה שבנצח

24 - הַיּוֹם אַרְבָּעָה וְעֶשְׂרִים יוֹם שֶׁהֵם
שְׁלֹשָׁה שָׁבוּעוֹת וּשְׁלֹשָׁה יָמִים לָעֹמֶר.
תפארת שבנצח

25 - הַיּוֹם חֲמִשָּׁה וְעֶשְׂרִים יוֹם שֶׁהֵם
שְׁלֹשָׁה שָׁבוּעוֹת וְאַרְבָּעָה יָמִים לָעֹמֶר.
נצח שבנצח

26 - הַיּוֹם שִׁשָּׁה וְעֶשְׂרִים יוֹם שֶׁהֵם
שְׁלֹשָׁה שָׁבוּעוֹת וַחֲמִשָּׁה יָמִים לָעֹמֶר.
הוד שבנצח

27 - הַיּוֹם שִׁבְעָה וְעֶשְׂרִים יוֹם שֶׁהֵם
שְׁלֹשָׁה שָׁבוּעוֹת וְשִׁשָּׁה יָמִים לָעֹמֶר.
יסוד שבנצח

28 - הַיּוֹם שְׁמוֹנָה וְעֶשְׂרִים יוֹם שֶׁהֵם
אַרְבָּעָה שָׁבוּעוֹת לָעֹמֶר.
מלכות שבנצח

Day 29: Ha-yom tish-öh v'esrim yom she-haym arbö-öh shövu-os v'yom echöd lö-omer.
(Chesed Sheb'hod)

Day 30: Ha-yom sh'loshim yom she-haym arbö-öh shövu-os ush'nay yömim lö-omer.
(G'vuröh Sheb'hod)

Day 31: Ha-yom echöd ush'loshim yom she-haym arbö-öh shövu-os ush'loshö yömim lö-omer.
(Tif-eres Sheb'hod)

Day 32: Ha-yom sh'na-yim ush'loshim yom she-haym arbö-öh shövu-os v'arbö-öh yömim lö-omer.
(Ne-tzach Sheb'hod)

Day 33: Ha-yom sh'loshöh ush'loshim yom she-haym arbö-öh shövu-os va-chamishöh yömim lö-omer.
(Hod Sheb'hod)

Day 34: Ha-yom arbö-öh ush'loshim yom she-haym arbö-öh shövu-os v'shishöh yömim lö-omer.
(Y'sod Sheb'hod)

Day 35: Ha-yom chamishöh ush'loshim yom she-haym chamishöh shövu-os lö-omer.
(Mal'chus Sheb'hod)

Day 36: Ha-yom shishö ush'loshim yom she-haym chamishöh shövu-os v'yom echöd lö-omer.
(Chesed Shebiy'sod)

Day 37: Ha-yom shiv-öh ush'loshim yom she-haym chamishöh shövu-os ush'nay yömim lö-omer.
(G'vuröh Shebiy'sod)

Day 38: Ha-yom sh'monöh ush'loshim yom she-haym chamishöh shövu-os ush'loshöh yömim lö-omer.
(Tif-eres Shebiy'sod)

Day 39: Ha-yom tish'öh ush'loshim yom she-haym chamishöh shövu-os v'arbö-öh yömim lö-omer.
(Ne-tzach Shebiy'sod)

29 - הַיּוֹם תִּשְׁעָה וְעֶשְׂרִים יוֹם שֶׁהֵם אַרְבָּעָה שָׁבוּעוֹת וְיוֹם אֶחָד לָעֹמֶר.
חסד שבהוד

30 - הַיּוֹם שְׁלֹשִׁים יוֹם שֶׁהֵם אַרְבָּעָה שָׁבוּעוֹת וּשְׁנֵי יָמִים לָעֹמֶר.
גבורה שבהוד

31 - הַיּוֹם אֶחָד וּשְׁלֹשִׁים יוֹם שֶׁהֵם אַרְבָּעָה שָׁבוּעוֹת וּשְׁלֹשָׁה יָמִים לָעֹמֶר.
תפארת שבהוד

32 - הַיּוֹם שְׁנַיִם וּשְׁלֹשִׁים יוֹם שֶׁהֵם אַרְבָּעָה שָׁבוּעוֹת וְאַרְבָּעָה יָמִים לָעֹמֶר.
נצח שבהוד

33 - הַיּוֹם שְׁלֹשָׁה וּשְׁלֹשִׁים יוֹם שֶׁהֵם אַרְבָּעָה שָׁבוּעוֹת וַחֲמִשָׁה יָמִים לָעֹמֶר.
הוד שבהוד

34 - הַיּוֹם אַרְבָּעָה וּשְׁלֹשִׁים יוֹם שֶׁהֵם אַרְבָּעָה שָׁבוּעוֹת וְשִׁשָׁה יָמִים לָעֹמֶר.
יסוד שבהוד

35 - הַיּוֹם חֲמִשָׁה וּשְׁלֹשִׁים יוֹם שֶׁהֵם חֲמִשָׁה שָׁבוּעוֹת לָעֹמֶר.
מלכות שבהוד

36 - הַיּוֹם שִׁשָׁה וּשְׁלֹשִׁים יוֹם שֶׁהֵם חֲמִשָׁה שָׁבוּעוֹת וְיוֹם אֶחָד לָעֹמֶר.
חסד שביסוד

37 - הַיּוֹם שִׁבְעָה וּשְׁלֹשִׁים יוֹם שֶׁהֵם חֲמִשָׁה שָׁבוּעוֹת וּשְׁנֵי יָמִים לָעֹמֶר.
גבורה שביסוד

38 - הַיּוֹם שְׁמוֹנָה וּשְׁלֹשִׁים יוֹם שֶׁהֵם חֲמִשָׁה שָׁבוּעוֹת וּשְׁלֹשָׁה יָמִים לָעֹמֶר.
תפארת שביסוד

39 - הַיּוֹם תִּשְׁעָה וּשְׁלֹשִׁים יוֹם שֶׁהֵם חֲמִשָׁה שָׁבוּעוֹת וְאַרְבָּעָה יָמִים לָעֹמֶר.
נצח שביסוד

Day 40: Ha-yom arbö-im yom she-haym
chamishöh shövu-os va-chamishöh yömim lö-omer.
(Hod Shebiy'sod)

Day 41: Hayom echöd v'arbö-im yom she-haym
chamishöh shövu-os v'shishöh yömim lö-omer.
(Y'sod Shebiy'sod)

Day 42: Ha-yom sh'na-yim v'arbö-im yom she-haym
shishöh shövu-os lö-omer.
(Mal'chus Shebiy'sod)

Day 43: Ha-yom sh'loshöh v'arbö-im yom she-haym
shishöh shövu-os v'yom echöd lö-omer.
(Chesed Sheb'mal'chus)

Day 44: Ha-yom arbö-öh v'arbö-im yom she-haym
shishöh shövu-os ush'nay yömim lö-omer.
(G'vuröh Sheb'mal'chus)

Day 45: Ha-yom chamishöh v'arbö-im yom she-haym
shishöh shövu-os ush'loshöh yömim lö-omer.
(Tif'eres Sheb'mal'chus)

Day 46: Ha-yom shishö v'arbö-im yom she-haym
shishöh shövu-os v'arbö-öh yömim lö-omer.
(Netzach Sheb'mal'chus)

Day 47: Ha-yom shiv-öh v'arbö-im yom she-haym
shishöh shövu-os va-chamishöh yömim lö-omer.
(Hod Sheb'mal'chus)

Day 48: Ha-yom sh'monöh v'arbö-im yom she-haym
shishöh shövu-os v'shishöh yömim lö-omer.
(Y'sod Sheb'mal'chus)

Day 49: Ha-yom tish'öh v'arbö-im yom she-haym
shiv'öh shövu-os lö-omer.
(Mal'chus Sheb'mal'chus)

40- הַיּוֹם אַרְבָּעִים יוֹם שֶׁהֵם
חֲמִשָּׁה שָׁבוּעוֹת וַחֲמִשָּׁה יָמִים לָעֹמֶר.
הוד שביסוד

41- הַיּוֹם אֶחָד וְאַרְבָּעִים יוֹם שֶׁהֵם
חֲמִשָּׁה שָׁבוּעוֹת וְשִׁשָּׁה יָמִים לָעֹמֶר.
יסוד שביסוד

42- הַיּוֹם שְׁנַיִם וְאַרְבָּעִים יוֹם שֶׁהֵם
שִׁשָּׁה שָׁבוּעוֹת לָעֹמֶר.
מלכות שביסוד

43- הַיּוֹם שְׁלֹשָׁה וְאַרְבָּעִים יוֹם שֶׁהֵם
שִׁשָּׁה שָׁבוּעוֹת וְיוֹם אֶחָד לָעֹמֶר.
חסד שבמלכות

44- הַיּוֹם אַרְבָּעָה וְאַרְבָּעִים יוֹם שֶׁהֵם
שִׁשָּׁה שָׁבוּעוֹת וּשְׁנֵי יָמִים לָעֹמֶר.
גבורה שבמלכות

45- הַיּוֹם חֲמִשָּׁה וְאַרְבָּעִים יוֹם שֶׁהֵם
שִׁשָּׁה שָׁבוּעוֹת וּשְׁלֹשָׁה יָמִים לָעֹמֶר.
תפארת שבמלכות

46- הַיּוֹם שִׁשָּׁה וְאַרְבָּעִים יוֹם שֶׁהֵם
שִׁשָּׁה שָׁבוּעוֹת וְאַרְבָּעָה יָמִים לָעֹמֶר.
נצח שבמלכות

47- הַיּוֹם שִׁבְעָה וְאַרְבָּעִים יוֹם שֶׁהֵם
שִׁשָּׁה שָׁבוּעוֹת וַחֲמִשָּׁה יָמִים לָעֹמֶר.
הוד שבמלכות

48- הַיּוֹם שְׁמוֹנָה וְאַרְבָּעִים יוֹם שֶׁהֵם
שִׁשָּׁה שָׁבוּעוֹת וְשִׁשָּׁה יָמִים לָעֹמֶר.
יסוד שבמלכות

49- הַיּוֹם תִּשְׁעָה וְאַרְבָּעִים יוֹם שֶׁהֵם
שִׁבְעָה שָׁבוּעוֹת לָעֹמֶר.
מלכות שבמלכות

Amidah for Passover, Shavuot, & Sukkot

The following *Amidah* is recited on the above festivals. When Shabbat occurs on the festivals we replace the regular Shabbat *Amidah* with the following, and include all parenthesized words.

Recited standing, with feet together:

אֲדֹנָי, שְׂפָתַי תִּפְתָּח וּפִי
Adonöy, s'fösai tif-töch u-fi

יַגִּיד תְּהִלָּתֶךָ:
yagid t'hilö-sechö.

My Lord, open my lips, and my mouth shall declare Your praise.

Take three steps back, and then three steps forward, as if one is approaching a king. At the words *"Boruch"* (blessed), bend the knee; at *"Atoh"* (You), bow forward; and at *"Adonoy"* (Lord), straighten up.

בָּרוּךְ אַתָּה יְיָ אֱלֹהֵינוּ
Böruch atöh adonöy elohaynu

וֵאלֹהֵי אֲבוֹתֵינוּ, אֱלֹהֵי אַבְרָהָם,
vay-lohay avosaynu, elohay avröhöm,

אֱלֹהֵי יִצְחָק, וֵאלֹהֵי יַעֲקֹב,
elohay yitzchök, vay-lohay ya-akov,

הָאֵל הַגָּדוֹל הַגִּבּוֹר וְהַנּוֹרָא,
hö-ayl ha-gödol ha-gibör, v'hanoröh,

אֵל עֶלְיוֹן, גּוֹמֵל חֲסָדִים טוֹבִים,
ayl el-yon, gomayl chasödim tovim,

קוֹנֵה הַכֹּל, וְזוֹכֵר חַסְדֵי
konay ha-kol, v'zochayr chas'day

אָבוֹת, וּמֵבִיא גוֹאֵל לִבְנֵי
övos, umayvi go-ayl liv'nay

בְנֵיהֶם לְמַעַן שְׁמוֹ בְּאַהֲבָה:
v'nayhem l'ma-an sh'mo b'ahavöh.

The Amidah for Festivals

At the words *"Boruch"* (blessed), bend the knee; at *"Atoh"* (You), bow forward; and at *"Adonoy"* (Lord), straighten up.

Melech ozayr umoshi-a umö-gayn.	מֶלֶךְ עוֹזֵר וּמוֹשִׁיעַ וּמָגֵן׃
Böruch atöh adonöy,	בָּרוּךְ אַתָּה יְיָ,
mögayn avröhöm.	מָגֵן אַבְרָהָם׃

Blessed are You, Lord our God and God of our fathers, God of Abraham, God of Isaac and God of Jacob, the great, mighty and awesome God, exalted God, who bestows bountiful kindness, who creates all things, who remembers the piety of the Patriarchs, and who, in love, brings a redeemer to their children's children, for the sake of His Name. O King, [You are] a helper, a savior and a shield. Blessed are You Lord, Shield of Abraham.

Atöh gibor l'olöm adonöy,	אַתָּה גִבּוֹר לְעוֹלָם אֲדֹנָי,
m'cha-yeh maysim atöh, rav l'hoshia.	מְחַיֶּה מֵתִים אַתָּה, רַב לְהוֹשִׁיעַ׃
In summer say: Morid ha-töl.	בקיץ׃ מוֹרִיד הַטָּל׃
In winter say: Mashiv höru-ach	בחורף׃ מַשִּׁיב הָרוּחַ
umorid ha-geshem.	וּמוֹרִיד הַגֶּשֶׁם׃
M'chalkayl cha-yim b'chesed,	מְכַלְכֵּל חַיִּים בְּחֶסֶד,
m'cha-yeh maysim b'rachamim	מְחַיֶּה מֵתִים בְּרַחֲמִים
rabim, somaych nof'lim, v'rofay	רַבִּים, סוֹמֵךְ נוֹפְלִים, וְרוֹפֵא
cholim, umatir asurim, um'ka-yaym	חוֹלִים, וּמַתִּיר אֲסוּרִים, וּמְקַיֵּם
emunöso lishaynay öför, mi	אֱמוּנָתוֹ לִישֵׁנֵי עָפָר, מִי
chömochö ba-al g'vuros umi do-meh	כָמוֹךָ בַּעַל גְּבוּרוֹת וּמִי דוֹמֶה
löch, melech maymis um'cha-yeh	לָךְ, מֶלֶךְ מֵמִית וּמְחַיֶּה

137

umatzmi-ach y'shuöh. : וּמַצְמִיחַ יְשׁוּעָה

V'ne-emön atöh l'ha-chayos maysim. : וְנֶאֱמָן אַתָּה לְהַחֲיוֹת מֵתִים

Boruch atöh adonöy, ,בָּרוּךְ אַתָּה יְיָ

m'cha-yeh ha-maysim. : מְחַיֵּה הַמֵּתִים

You are mighty forever, my Lord; You resurrect the dead; You are powerful to save. (In summer say: He causes the dew to descend.) (In winter say: He causes the wind to blow and the rain to fall.) He sustains the living with loving-kindness, resurrects the dead with great mercy, supports the falling, heals the sick, releases the bound, and fulfills His trust to those who sleep in the dust. Who is like You, mighty One! And who can be compared to You, King, who brings death and restores life, and causes deliverance to spring forth! You are trustworthy to revive the dead. Blessed are You Lord, who revives the dead.

Atöh ködosh v'shim'chö ködosh אַתָּה קָדוֹשׁ וְשִׁמְךָ קָדוֹשׁ

uk'doshim b'chöl yom y'hal'luchö וּקְדוֹשִׁים בְּכָל יוֹם יְהַלְלוּךָ

selöh. Boruch atöh adonöy, ,סֶלָה : בָּרוּךְ אַתָּה יְיָ

hö-ayl ha-ködosh. : הָאֵל הַקָּדוֹשׁ

You are holy and Your Name is holy, and holy beings praise You daily for all eternity. Blessed are You Lord, the holy God.

Atöh v'chartönu miköl hö-amim, ,אַתָּה בְחַרְתָּנוּ מִכָּל הָעַמִּים

öhavtö osönu v'rö-tzisö bönu, ,אָהַבְתָּ אוֹתָנוּ וְרָצִיתָ בָּנוּ

v'ro-mamtönu miköl ha-l'shonos, ,וְרוֹמַמְתָּנוּ מִכָּל הַלְּשׁוֹנוֹת

v'kidash-tönu b'mitz-vosechö, ,וְקִדַּשְׁתָּנוּ בְּמִצְוֹתֶיךָ

v'kayrav-tönu malkaynu וְקֵרַבְתָּנוּ מַלְכֵּנוּ

la-avodö-sechö, v'shim'chö לַעֲבֹדָתֶךָ, וְשִׁמְךָ

ha-gödol v'haködosh ölaynu körösö: הַגָּדוֹל וְהַקָּדוֹשׁ עָלֵינוּ קָרָאתָ

You have chosen us from among all the nations; You have loved us and found favor with us. You have raised us above all tongues and made us holy through Your commandments. You, our King, have drawn us near to Your service and proclaimed Your great and holy Name upon us.

When the festival falls on Saturday night, add the following:

Vatodi-aynu adonöy elohaynu וַתּוֹדִיעֵנוּ יְיָ אֱלֹהֵינוּ

es mish-p'tay tzidkechö, אֶת מִשְׁפְּטֵי צִדְקֶךָ,

vat'lam'daynu la-asos chukay וַתְּלַמְּדֵנוּ לַעֲשׂוֹת חֻקֵּי

r'tzonechö. Vati-ten lönu, adonöy רְצוֹנֶךָ. וַתִּתֶּן לָנוּ, יְיָ

elohaynu, mishpötim y'shörim v'soros אֱלֹהֵינוּ, מִשְׁפָּטִים יְשָׁרִים וְתוֹרוֹת

emes, chukim umitzvos tovim, אֱמֶת, חֻקִּים וּמִצְוֹת טוֹבִים,

vatan-chilaynu z'manay söson וַתַּנְחִילֵנוּ זְמַנֵּי שָׂשׂוֹן

umo-aday kodesh v'chagay n'dövöh, וּמוֹעֲדֵי קֹדֶשׁ וְחַגֵּי נְדָבָה,

vatori-shaynu k'dushas shabös וַתּוֹרִישֵׁנוּ קְדֻשַּׁת שַׁבָּת

uch'vod mo-ayd va-chagigas höregel, וּכְבוֹד מוֹעֵד וַחֲגִיגַת הָרָגֶל,

vatavdayl adonöy elohaynu bayn וַתַּבְדֵּל יְיָ אֱלֹהֵינוּ בֵּין

kodesh l'chol, bayn or l'choshech, קֹדֶשׁ לְחוֹל, בֵּין אוֹר לְחשֶׁךְ,

bayn yisrö-ayl lö-amim, bayn yom בֵּין יִשְׂרָאֵל לָעַמִּים, בֵּין יוֹם

ha-sh'vi-i l'shayshes y'may hama-aseh. הַשְּׁבִיעִי לְשֵׁשֶׁת יְמֵי הַמַּעֲשֶׂה,

Bayn k'dushas shabös lik'dushas בֵּין קְדֻשַּׁת שַׁבָּת לִקְדֻשַּׁת

yom tov hivdaltö, v'es yom ha-sh'vi-i יוֹם טוֹב הִבְדַּלְתָּ. וְאֶת יוֹם הַשְּׁבִיעִי

mi-shayshes y'may ha-ma-aseh מִשֵּׁשֶׁת יְמֵי הַמַּעֲשֶׂה
kidashtö, hivdaltö v'kidashtö es קִדַּשְׁתָּ. הִבְדַּלְתָּ וְקִדַּשְׁתָּ אֶת
am'chö yisrö-ayl bik'dushösechö. עַמְּךָ יִשְׂרָאֵל בִּקְדֻשָּׁתֶךָ:

You, Lord our God, have made known to us Your righteous statutes and taught us to carry out the decrees of Your will. You, Lord our God, have given us just statutes and teachings of truth, decrees and precepts that are good. You have given us as a heritage joyous seasons, holy festivals and holidays for [bringing] voluntary offerings. You have bequeathed to us the holiness of the Shabbat, the glory of the holiday and the celebration of the festival. You, Lord our God, have made a distinction between sacred and profane, between light and darkness, between Israel and the nations, between the Seventh Day and the six work days; between the holiness of the Shabbat and the holiness of the Festival You have made a distinction, and have sanctified the Seventh Day above the six work days. You have set apart and sanctified Your people Israel with Your holiness.

Vatiten lönu adonöy elohaynu וַתִּתֶּן לָנוּ יְיָ אֱלֹהֵינוּ
b'ahavöh (shabösos lim'nuchöh u-) בְּאַהֲבָה (שַׁבָּתוֹת לִמְנוּחָה וּ)
mo-adim l'simchöh chagim מוֹעֲדִים לְשִׂמְחָה חַגִּים
uz'manim l'söson es yom וּזְמַנִּים לְשָׂשׂוֹן אֶת יוֹם
(ha-shabös ha-zeh v'es yom) (הַשַּׁבָּת הַזֶּה וְאֶת יוֹם)
on Passover: לפסח:
chag ha-matzos ha-zeh, חַג הַמַּצּוֹת הַזֶּה,
on Shavuot: לשבועות:
chag ha-shövu-os ha-zeh חַג הַשָּׁבוּעוֹת הַזֶּה

The Amidah for Festivals

on Sukkot:	לסוכות :
chag ha-sukos ha-zeh	חַג הַסֻּכּוֹת הַזֶּה
on Shmini Atzeret and	לשמיני עצרת
Simchat Torah:	ולשמחת תורה :
sh'mini atzeres ha-chag ha-zeh	שְׁמִינִי עֲצֶרֶת הַחַג הַזֶּה
V'es yom tov mikrö kodesh	וְאֶת יוֹם טוֹב מִקְרָא קֹדֶשׁ
ha-zeh, z'man	הַזֶּה, זְמַן
on Passover:	לפסח :
chayru-saynu	חֵרוּתֵנוּ
on Shavuot:	לשבועות :
matan torö-saynu	מַתַּן תּוֹרָתֵנוּ
on Sukkot:	לסוכות :
simchö-saynu	שִׂמְחָתֵנוּ
on Shmini Atzeret and	לשמיני עצרת
Simchat Torah:	ולשמחת תורה :
simchö-saynu	שִׂמְחָתֵנוּ
(b'ahavöh) mikrö kodesh zaycher	(בְּאַהֲבָה) מִקְרָא קֹדֶשׁ זֵכֶר
litzi-as mitzrö-yim.	לִיצִיאַת מִצְרָיִם.

And You, Lord our God, have given us in love (**On Shabbat:** *Sabbaths for rest and*) *festivals for rejoicing, holidays and seasons for gladness,* (**On Shabbat:** *this Shabbat day and*) *this day of:* (**On Passover:** *the Festival of Matzos, and this festival of holy assembly, the*

season of our freedom), (**On Shavuot:** *the Festival of Shavuot, and this festival of holy assembly, the season of the giving of our Torah*), (**On Sukkot:** *the Festival of Sukkot, and this festival of holy assembly, the season of our rejoicing*), (**On Shmini Atzeret and Simchat Torah:** *Shmini Atzeret the Festival, and this festival of holy assembly, the season of our rejoicing*), (**On Shabbat:** *in love,*) a holy assembly, commemorating the Exodus from Egypt.

Elohaynu vay-lohay avosaynu	אֱלֹהֵינוּ וֵאלֹהֵי אֲבוֹתֵינוּ
ya-aleh v'yövo, v'yagi-a v'yayrö-eh	יַעֲלֶה וְיָבֹא, וְיַגִּיעַ וְיֵרָאֶה
v'yayrö-tzeh, v'yishöma v'yipökayd	וְיֵרָצֶה, וְיִשָּׁמַע וְיִפָּקֵד
v'yizöchayr, zichro-naynu	וְיִזָּכֵר, זִכְרוֹנֵנוּ
ufik'do-naynu, v'zichron	וּפִקְדוֹנֵנוּ, וְזִכְרוֹן
avosaynu, v'zichron möshi-ach	אֲבוֹתֵינוּ, וְזִכְרוֹן מָשִׁיחַ
ben dövid avdechö, v'zichron	בֶּן דָּוִד עַבְדֶּךָ, וְזִכְרוֹן
y'rushöla-yim ir köd-shechö,	יְרוּשָׁלַיִם עִיר קָדְשֶׁךָ,
v'zichron köl am'chö bays yisrö-ayl	וְזִכְרוֹן כָּל עַמְּךָ בֵּית יִשְׂרָאֵל
l'fönechö lif'laytöh l'tovöh, l'chayn	לְפָנֶיךָ לִפְלֵיטָה לְטוֹבָה, לְחֵן
ul'chesed ul'rachamim ul'cha-yim	וּלְחֶסֶד וּלְרַחֲמִים וּלְחַיִּים
tovim ul'shölom b'yom	טוֹבִים וּלְשָׁלוֹם, בְּיוֹם

(ha-shabös ha-zeh uv'yom)	(הַשַּׁבָּת הַזֶּה וּבְיוֹם)
On Passover:	לפסח:
chag ha-matzos ha-zeh,	חַג הַמַּצּוֹת הַזֶּה
On Shavuot:	לשבועות:
chag ha-shövu-os ha-zeh	חַג הַשָּׁבוּעוֹת הַזֶּה

The Amidah for Festivals

<table>
<tr><td>On Sukkot:</td><td>לסוכות:</td></tr>
<tr><td>chag ha-sukos ha-zeh</td><td>חַג הַסֻּכּוֹת הַזֶּה</td></tr>
<tr><td>On Shmini Atzeret and</td><td>לשמיני עצרת</td></tr>
<tr><td>Simchat Torah:</td><td>ולשמחת תורה:</td></tr>
<tr><td>sh'mini atzeres ha-chag ha-zeh,</td><td>שְׁמִינִי עֲצֶרֶת הַחַג הַזֶּה,</td></tr>
</table>

<table>
<tr><td>b'yom tov mikrö kodesh ha-zeh:</td><td>בְּיוֹם טוֹב מִקְרָא קֹדֶשׁ הַזֶּה:</td></tr>
<tr><td>Zöch'raynu adonöy elohaynu bo</td><td>זָכְרֵנוּ יְיָ אֱלֹהֵינוּ בּוֹ</td></tr>
<tr><td>l'tovöh, ufök'daynu vo liv'röchöh,</td><td>לְטוֹבָה, וּפָקְדֵנוּ בוֹ לִבְרָכָה,</td></tr>
<tr><td>v'hoshi-aynu vo l'cha-yim tovim.</td><td>וְהוֹשִׁיעֵנוּ בוֹ לְחַיִּים טוֹבִים:</td></tr>
<tr><td>Uvid'var y'shu-öh v'rachamim</td><td>וּבִדְבַר יְשׁוּעָה וְרַחֲמִים</td></tr>
<tr><td>chus v'chönaynu v'rachaym ölaynu</td><td>חוּס וְחָנֵּנוּ וְרַחֵם עָלֵינוּ</td></tr>
<tr><td>v'hoshi-aynu ki aylechö aynaynu,</td><td>וְהוֹשִׁיעֵנוּ כִּי אֵלֶיךָ עֵינֵינוּ,</td></tr>
<tr><td>ki ayl melech chanun</td><td>כִּי אֵל מֶלֶךְ חַנּוּן</td></tr>
<tr><td>v'rachum ötöh.</td><td>וְרַחוּם אָתָּה:</td></tr>
</table>

Our God and God of our fathers, may there ascend, come and reach, be seen, accepted, and heard, recalled and remembered before You, the remembrance and recollection of us, the remembrance of our fathers, the remembrance of Moshiach the son of David Your servant, the remembrance of Jerusalem Your holy city, and the remembrance of all Your people the House of Israel, for deliverance, well-being, grace, kindness, mercy, good life and peace, on this day of: (**On Passover:** *the Festival of Matzot,*) (**On Shavuot:** *the Festival of Shavuot,*) (**On Sukkot:** *the Festival of Sukkot,*) (**On Shmini Atzeret and Simchat Torah:** *Shmini Atzeret, the Festival,*) *on this holy Festival day. Remember us on this [day], Lord our God, for good; be mindful of us on this [day] for blessing; help us on this [day] for good life. With*

the promise of deliverance and compassion, spare us and be gracious to us; have mercy upon us and deliver us; for our eyes are directed to You, for You, God, are a gracious and merciful King.

V'hasi-aynu adonöy elohaynu es birkas mo-adechö. L'cha-yim tovim ul'shölom, l'simchöh ul'söson, ka-asher rö-tzisöh v'ömarto l'vö-r'chaynu. (Elohaynu vay-lohay avosaynu, r'tzay nö vim'nuchösaynu), kad'shaynu b'mitzvosechö v'sayn chel-kaynu b'sorösechö, sab'aynu mituvechö v'samay-ach naf-shaynu bishu-ösechö, v'tahayr libaynu l'öv-d'chö be-emes, v'han-chi-laynu adonöy elohaynu (b'ahavöh uv'rötzon) b'simchöh uv'söson, (shabös u-) mo-aday köd-shechö, v'yis-m'chu v'chö köl yisrö-ayl m'kadshay sh'mechö. Boruch atöh adonöy, m'kadaysh (ha-shabös v') yisrö-ayl v'haz'manim.

וְהַשִׂיאֵנוּ יְיָ אֱלֹהֵינוּ אֶת בִּרְכַּת מוֹעֲדֶיךָ: לְחַיִּים טוֹבִים וּלְשָׁלוֹם, לְשִׂמְחָה וּלְשָׂשׂוֹן, כַּאֲשֶׁר רָצִיתָ וְאָמַרְתָּ לְבָרְכֵנוּ. (אֱלֹהֵינוּ וֵאלֹהֵי אֲבוֹתֵינוּ רְצֵה נָא בִמְנוּחָתֵנוּ) קַדְּשֵׁנוּ בְּמִצְוֹתֶיךָ, וְתֵן חֶלְקֵנוּ בְּתוֹרָתֶךָ, שַׂבְּעֵנוּ מִטּוּבֶךָ, וְשַׂמַּח נַפְשֵׁנוּ בִּישׁוּעָתֶךָ, וְטַהֵר לִבֵּנוּ לְעָבְדְּךָ בֶּאֱמֶת, וְהַנְחִילֵנוּ יְיָ אֱלֹהֵינוּ (בְּאַהֲבָה וּבְרָצוֹן) בְּשִׂמְחָה וּבְשָׂשׂוֹן (שַׁבָּת וּ) מוֹעֲדֵי קָדְשֶׁךָ, וְיִשְׂמְחוּ בְךָ כָּל יִשְׂרָאֵל מְקַדְּשֵׁי שְׁמֶךָ. בָּרוּךְ אַתָּה יְיָ, מְקַדֵּשׁ (הַשַּׁבָּת וְ) יִשְׂרָאֵל וְהַזְּמַנִּים:

Bestow upon us, Lord our God, the blessings of Your festivals for good life and for peace, for joy and for gladness, as You desired and promised to bless us. (On Shabbat: Our God and God of our fathers, please find favor in our rest.) Make us holy with Your

144

*commandments and grant us our portion in Your Torah; satiate us with Your goodness, gladden our soul with Your salvation, and make our heart pure to serve You in truth. Lord our God, grant as our heritage, (**On Shabbat:** in love and goodwill,) in joy and gladness, Your holy (**On Shabbat:** Shabbat and) Festivals, and may all Israel who sanctify Your Name rejoice in You. Blessed are You Lord, who sanctifies (**On Shabbat:** the Shabbat and) Israel and the [festive] seasons.*

R'tzay, adonöy elohaynu, b'am'chö	רְצֵה, יְיָ אֱלֹהֵינוּ, בְּעַמְּךָ
yisrö-ayl, v'lis'filösöm sh'ay, v'höshayv	יִשְׂרָאֵל, וְלִתְפִלָּתָם שְׁעֵה, וְהָשֵׁב
hö-avodöh lid'vir baysechö, v'ishay	הָעֲבוֹדָה לִדְבִיר בֵּיתֶךָ, וְאִשֵּׁי
yisrö-ayl us'filösöm b'ahavöh	יִשְׂרָאֵל וּתְפִלָּתָם בְּאַהֲבָה
s'kabayl b'rö-tzon, us'hi l'rö-tzon	תְקַבֵּל בְּרָצוֹן, וּתְהִי לְרָצוֹן
tömid avodas yisrö-ayl amechö.	תָּמִיד עֲבוֹדַת יִשְׂרָאֵל עַמֶּךָ:

Look with favor, Lord our God, on Your people Israel and pay heed to their prayer; restore the service to Your Sanctuary and accept with love and favor Israel's fire-offerings and prayer; and may the service of Your people Israel always find favor.

V'se-chezenöh aynaynu	וְתֶחֱזֶינָה עֵינֵינוּ
b'shuv'chö l'tziyon b'rachamim.	בְּשׁוּבְךָ לְצִיּוֹן בְּרַחֲמִים.
Böruch atöh adonöy, ha-machazir	בָּרוּךְ אַתָּה יְיָ, הַמַּחֲזִיר
sh'chinöso l'tziyon.	שְׁכִינָתוֹ לְצִיּוֹן:

May our eyes behold Your return to Zion in mercy. Blessed are You Lord, who restores His Divine Presence to Zion.

Bow forward when saying the first five words of *Modim* (We thankfully).

Modim anachnu löch, shö-atöh hu מוֹדִים אֲנַחְנוּ לָךְ, שָׁאַתָּה הוּא

adonöy elohaynu vay-lohay avosaynu יְיָ אֱלֹהֵינוּ וֵאלֹהֵי אֲבוֹתֵינוּ

l'olöm vö-ed, tzur cha-yaynu mögayn לְעוֹלָם וָעֶד, צוּר חַיֵּינוּ מָגֵן

yish-aynu, atöh hu l'dor vödor, יִשְׁעֵנוּ, אַתָּה הוּא לְדוֹר וָדוֹר,

no-deh l'chö un'sapayr t'hilösechö, נוֹדֶה לְּךָ וּנְסַפֵּר תְּהִלָּתֶךָ,

al cha-yaynu ha-m'surim b'yödechö, עַל חַיֵּינוּ הַמְּסוּרִים בְּיָדֶךָ,

v'al nish'mosaynu ha-p'kudos löch, וְעַל נִשְׁמוֹתֵינוּ הַפְּקוּדוֹת לָךְ,

v'al nisechö sheb'chöl yom imönu, וְעַל נִסֶּיךָ שֶׁבְּכָל יוֹם עִמָּנוּ,

v'al nif-l'ösechö v'tovosechö sheb'chöl וְעַל נִפְלְאוֹתֶיךָ וְטוֹבוֹתֶיךָ שֶׁבְּכָל

ays erev vövoker v'tzöhörö-yim, עֵת, עֶרֶב וָבֹקֶר וְצָהֳרָיִם,

ha-tov, ki lo chölu ra-chamechö, הַטּוֹב, כִּי לֹא כָלוּ רַחֲמֶיךָ,

v'ham'rachaym, ki lo samu וְהַמְרַחֵם, כִּי לֹא תַמּוּ

chasödechö, ki may-olöm kivinu löch. חֲסָדֶיךָ, כִּי מֵעוֹלָם קִוִּינוּ לָךְ:

We thankfully acknowledge that You are the Lord our God and God of our fathers forever. You are the strength of our life, the shield of our salvation in every generation. We will give thanks to You and recount Your praise, evening, morning and noon, for our lives which are committed into Your hand, for our souls which are entrusted to You, for Your miracles which are with us daily, and for Your continual wonders and beneficences. You are the Beneficent One, for Your mercies never cease; and the Merciful One, for Your kindnesses never end; for we always place our hope in You.

V'al kulöm yisböraych v'yisromöm וְעַל כֻּלָּם יִתְבָּרַךְ וְיִתְרוֹמַם

v'yis-nasay shim'chö malkaynu וְיִתְנַשֵּׂא שִׁמְךָ מַלְכֵּנוּ

tömid l'olöm vö-ed. תָּמִיד לְעוֹלָם וָעֶד:

The Amidah for Festivals

And for all these, may Your Name, our King, be continually blessed, exalted and extolled forever and all time.

At the words "Boruch" (blessed), bend the knee; at "Atoh" (You), bow forward; and at "Adonoy" (Lord), straighten up.

V'chöl ha-cha-yim yo-duchö selöh
vihal'lu shim'chö ha-gödol l'olöm ki
tov, hö-ayl y'shu-ösaynu v'ezrösaynu
selöh, hö-ayl ha-tov. Boruch atöh
adonöy, ha-tov shim'chö ul'chö
nö-eh l'hodos.

וְכָל הַחַיִּים יוֹדוּךָ סֶּלָה
וִיהַלְלוּ שִׁמְךָ הַגָּדוֹל לְעוֹלָם כִּי
טוֹב, הָאֵל יְשׁוּעָתֵנוּ וְעֶזְרָתֵנוּ
סֶלָה, הָאֵל הַטּוֹב. בָּרוּךְ אַתָּה
יְיָ, הַטּוֹב שִׁמְךָ וּלְךָ
נָאֶה לְהוֹדוֹת:

And all living things shall forever thank You, and praise Your great Name eternally, for You are good. God, You are our everlasting salvation and help, O benevolent God. Blessed are You Lord, Beneficent is Your Name, and to You it is fitting to offer thanks.

Sim shölom tovöh uv'röchöh,
cha-yim chayn vöchesed v'rachamim,
ölaynu v'al köl yisrö-ayl amechö.
Bö-r'chaynu övinu kulönu k'echöd
b'or pönechö, ki v'or pönechö,
nösatö lönu, adonöy elohaynu,
toras cha-yim v'ahavas chesed
utz'dököh uv'röchöh v'rachamim
v'cha-yim v'shölom. V'tov b'aynechö
l'voraych es am'chö yisrö-ayl b'chöl

שִׂים שָׁלוֹם, טוֹבָה וּבְרָכָה,
חַיִּים חֵן וָחֶסֶד וְרַחֲמִים,
עָלֵינוּ וְעַל כָּל יִשְׂרָאֵל עַמֶּךָ:
בָּרְכֵנוּ אָבִינוּ כֻּלָּנוּ כְּאֶחָד
בְּאוֹר פָּנֶיךָ, כִּי בְאוֹר פָּנֶיךָ,
נָתַתָּ לָנוּ יְיָ אֱלֹהֵינוּ
תּוֹרַת חַיִּים, וְאַהֲבַת חֶסֶד
וּצְדָקָה וּבְרָכָה וְרַחֲמִים
וְחַיִּים וְשָׁלוֹם: וְטוֹב בְּעֵינֶיךָ
לְבָרֵךְ אֶת עַמְּךָ יִשְׂרָאֵל בְּכָל

147

ays uv'chöl shö-öh bish'lomechö. : עֵת וּבְכָל שָׁעָה בִּשְׁלוֹמֶךָ

Boruch atöh adonöy, ha-m'vöraych es בָּרוּךְ אַתָּה יְיָ, הַמְבָרֵךְ אֶת

amo yisrö-ayl ba-shölom. : עַמּוֹ יִשְׂרָאֵל בַּשָׁלוֹם

Bestow peace, goodness and blessing, life, graciousness, kindness and mercy, upon us and upon all Your people Israel. Bless us, our Father, all of us as one, with the light of Your countenance. For by the light of Your countenance You gave us, Lord our God, the Torah of life and loving-kindness, righteousness, blessing, mercy, life and peace. May it be favorable in Your eyes to bless Your people Israel, at all times and at every moment, with Your peace. Blessed are You Lord, who blesses His people Israel with peace.

Yih-yu l'rö-tzon im'ray fi, v'heg-yon יִהְיוּ לְרָצוֹן אִמְרֵי פִי, וְהֶגְיוֹן

libi l'fönechö, adonöy tzuri v'go-ali. : לִבִּי לְפָנֶיךָ, יְיָ צוּרִי וְגוֹאֲלִי

May the words of my mouth and the meditation of my heart be acceptable before You, Lord, my Strength and my Redeemer.

Elohai, n'tzor l'shoni may-rö, us'fösai אֱלֹהַי, נְצוֹר לְשׁוֹנִי מֵרָע, וּשְׂפָתַי

midabayr mirmöh. V'lim'kal'lai, מִדַבֵּר מִרְמָה : וְלִמְקַלְלַי,

nafshi sidom, v'nafshi ke-öför la-kol נַפְשִׁי תִדּוֹם, וְנַפְשִׁי כֶּעָפָר לַכֹּל

tih-yeh. P'sach libi b'sorösechö, תִּהְיֶה : פְּתַח לִבִּי בְּתוֹרָתֶךָ,

uv'mitzvosechö tirdof nafshi, וּבְמִצְוֹתֶיךָ תִּרְדוֹף נַפְשִׁי,

v'chöl ha-chosh'vim ölai rö-öh, וְכָל הַחוֹשְׁבִים עָלַי רָעָה,

m'hayröh höfayr atzösöm v'kalkayl מְהֵרָה הָפֵר עֲצָתָם וְקַלְקֵל

ma-chashavtöm. Yih-yu k'motz lif'nay מַחֲשַׁבְתָּם : יִהְיוּ כְּמוֹץ לִפְנֵי

ru-ach umal'ach adonöy do-cheh. : רוּחַ וּמַלְאַךְ יְיָ דוֹחֶה

The Amidah for Festivals

L'ma-an yay-chöl'tzun y'didechö, לְמַעַן יֵחָלְצוּן יְדִידֶיךָ,
hoshi-öh y'min'chö va-anayni. הוֹשִׁיעָה יְמִינְךָ וַעֲנֵנִי.
Asay l'ma-an sh'mechö, asay l'ma-an עֲשֵׂה לְמַעַן שְׁמֶךָ, עֲשֵׂה לְמַעַן
y'minechö, asay l'ma-an torösechö, יְמִינֶךָ, עֲשֵׂה לְמַעַן תּוֹרָתֶךָ.
asay l'ma-an k'dusho-sechö. עֲשֵׂה לְמַעַן קְדֻשָּׁתֶךָ.

Yih-yu l'rö-tzon im'ray fi, v'heg-yon יִהְיוּ לְרָצוֹן אִמְרֵי פִי, וְהֶגְיוֹן
libi l'fönechö, adonöy tzuri v'go-ali. לִבִּי לְפָנֶיךָ, יְיָ צוּרִי וְגוֹאֲלִי.

My God, guard my tongue from evil and my lips from speaking deceitfully. Let my soul be silent to those who curse me; let my soul be as dust to all. Open my heart to Your Torah, and let my soul eagerly pursue Your commandments. As for all those who plot evil against me, hasten to annul their counsel and frustrate their design. Let them be as chaff before the wind; let the angel of the Lord thrust them away. That Your beloved ones may be delivered, help with Your right hand and answer me. Do it for the sake of Your Name; do it for the sake of Your right hand; do it for the sake of Your Torah; do it for the sake of Your holiness. May the words of my mouth and the meditation of my heart be acceptable before You, Lord, my Strength and my Redeemer.

Take three steps back and say:

O-seh shölom bim'romöv, hu עֹשֶׂה שָׁלוֹם בִּמְרוֹמָיו, הוּא
ya-aseh shölom ölaynu v'al köl יַעֲשֶׂה שָׁלוֹם עָלֵינוּ וְעַל כָּל
yisrö-ayl, v'im'ru ömayn. יִשְׂרָאֵל, וְאִמְרוּ אָמֵן:

He who makes peace in His heavens, may He make peace for us and for all Israel; and say: Amen.

149

Y'hi rö-tzon mil'fönechö, adonöy יְהִי רָצוֹן מִלְּפָנֶיךָ, יְיָ
elohaynu vay-löhay avosaynu, אֱלֹהֵינוּ וֵאלֹהֵי אֲבוֹתֵינוּ,
she-yibö-neh bays ha-mikdösh שֶׁיִּבָּנֶה בֵּית הַמִּקְדָּשׁ
bim'hayröh v'yömaynu, v'sayn בִּמְהֵרָה בְיָמֵינוּ, וְתֵן
chelkaynu b'sorösechö. חֶלְקֵנוּ בְּתוֹרָתֶךָ.

May it be Your will, Lord our God and God of our fathers, that the Beit Hamikdash (Holy Temple) be speedily rebuilt in our days, and grant us our portion in Your Torah.

Take three steps forward.
This concludes the Festival Amidah

Where to next?

On Shavuot and Sukkot: The Amidah is followed by Whole Kaddish and *Olaynu* (It is Incumbent...), on page 111, 116.

On Shabbat: Continue with "*Vayechulu*" (The Heavens...), on page 108.

On the first night of Passover: Add the whole *Hallel* (not included here).

On the second night of Passover: Add the whole *Hallel* (not included here), and the Counting of the first night of the Omer, on page 127.

Inspirational Reading

"Spiritual Warrior"
By Jay Litvin

Frankly I loathe being called a "religious" person. It sounds so boring. I'm reminded of a person who once told me how much he envied me. "Life for you is so simple," he said. "Your religion tells you what to do and what not to do, and gives you all the answers."

Boy, I wish.

But, in truth, this is what the word "religion" conjures up: something kind of old and staid, perhaps even a bit crusty. Something calm and peaceful, barely alive and never in motion.

And so I reject the title of "religious person." I'm just a guy who looks like a religious person.

So then, what am I?

Well, in truth, life feels more to me like a battleground than a prayer service, and my inner reality is more that of a warrior than a pious person.

So, if I have to label myself anything (which I vigorously avoid doing), I would have to call myself a "spiritual warrior." And here's what that means for me.

A warrior is one who enters the battlefield with a healthy dose of fear and a larger dose of love. He fights for a principle or for his country or for his king, and his love for these outweighs the fear he feels for his own safety. He requires courage and skill, for he risks his very life.

A warrior loves the battlefield; it is here that he is most alive. He must at all times act with his full awareness and ability; even the slightest lapse will cause his downfall.

The battlefield brings forth from the warrior capabilities and potentials that he didn't even know existed within himself. And so, as he fights, he is in a constant state of self-discovery.

The true warrior longs for the battlefield, for the rest of life seems, in comparison, like a place where he is able to actualize only a small part of who he is. So he craves the challenge and the encounter. He loves living on the edge. It is here that he is the most of who he is, and where he discovers that he is, in fact, more than who he thinks he is.

Living as a Jew and a chassid is this experience. It is an encounter with the Almighty and with myself. It is the place of self-discovery and challenge. It requires the bravery of facing who I am and who I am not. It takes a willingness to see the potential of who I can be and face the smallness of who I have allowed myself to be.

When I am living Jewishly, I am living at the edge. I am in a no-man's land where each encounter, each moment, presents an opportunity to learn, to act, to refine and to transform. Sometimes, like King Arthur, I am battling dragons within and without; sometimes I am challenged by beasts that threaten to devour me with their anger and

fear; sometimes I am fighting for my own sanity, attempting to reconcile the tactual world with a world which can neither be seen, heard or touched.

As a spiritual warrior — when I am blessed to be living smack in the middle of the battlefield — I am fully alive, wrestling at the edge of who I am. It matters not whether I am in prayer, giving my child a bath, or sitting at my computer. The battlefield includes my personal relationships, my inner desires, my overdrawn bank account, and my constant lack of sleep. It embraces my marriage and employment. My frustration, patience, envy, lust and greed. It is a state of mind, a willingness to find God in all places and to meet Him fully, allowing Him to penetrate into the deepest recesses of who I am and to dispel all the images of who I think I am.

Each time, and there are many such times, that I confront the imperative of what I must do with the reluctance of what I want to do; each time that I must transform thoughts and attitudes formed through years of life and conditioning into holy thoughts and holy attitudes, I am on the battlefield. Whether it's giving charity from the few pennies left in the coffer, or taking on an additional responsibility, or offering to help a friend or not even a friend when I can barely stay awake, I am on the battlefield. When tragedy strikes my family, God forbid, and I must discover a way to be both genuine with my grief and yet remain cognizant of the good I know that God gives to the world, I am being a spiritual warrior.

As a spiritual warrior I discover my faith when I am at the limits of my faith. I find my love of God when I am angry with God. I find my

trust in the Protector of the world when I am at my most frightened. And I find my obedience to the Almighty when I feel the most rebellious.

I am a spiritual warrior when I fully feel my despair, and find the hope to go on. When I feel betrayed, yet discover my trust. When I reach higher than I should, then fail and fall, only to discover that I have landed at a station higher than the one from which I reached.

On this battlefield called *Yiddishkeit*, I am stretched to the limit only to find that my limit is nowhere near what I thought it was. I am alive and growing, moving, in process. Scared and exhilarated. Craving victory and having not the slightest idea of what it means.

To me, all the rest, as Rabbi Schneur Zalman of Liadi says in his *Tanya*, is conceit. To be despondent over the fact that I am constantly in the midst of a struggle is to pretend that I am something more than who I really am. It is to pretend that I am a *tzaddik*, one of the righteous few who have vanquished the negative within themselves, when in fact I can only aspire, at my best moments, to the level of beinoni, the spiritual warrior in the battlefield of life.

The *Tanya* tells us to rejoice when we are challenged within or without because this is our task: to enter the battlefield. We are, it seems to me, like soldiers who have trained endlessly for battle, and shout in joy when the moment finally arrives to test their abilities and find the real stuff of which they are made.

And this is the spiritual warrior's challenge: to find the stuff of which he is made, whether it is to his liking or not, and bring himself fully into the struggle with himself and his encounter with God.

I find this battle terrifying, because I have no idea where it will lead. It forces me to open myself to God and allow Him into the innermost, most intimate confines of myself. It forces me to confront the plaguing question: If I truly let God in, what will He do to me once He is there? Who will I be? What will the world have become? And what is my place and purpose within it?

Religious? Me? Hardly. A Torah life is no place for a religious person. Religion is much too safe for such a journey into the unknown, into a meeting place with God. Only a warrior can embrace such a task.

Synagogue Glossary

Aliyah: Being called up to the Torah.
Amen (lit., "true"): Acknowledgement.
Amidah (lit., "standing"): Silent Prayer.
Amud (lit., "stand"): Prayer stand.
Aron Kodesh (lit., "holy ark"): Ark where the Torah is stored.
Becher (Yiddish): Cup used for Kiddush.
Besamim: Fragrant spices used for Havdalah.
Bimah (lit., "stage"): Reading Table.
Birkat Hagomel: Thanksgiving blessing.
Birkat Kohanim: Preistly Blessing.
Chazzan (lit., "cantor"): Prayer Leader.
Ezrat Noshim: Women Section.
Gabbai: Organizer; assistant.
Gartel (Yiddish): Tie for the Torah; special prayer belt.
Gellilah: Binding the Torah.
Genizah: Repository of worn Hebrew texts.
Haftorah: Portion from the Prophets.
Hagboh: Lifting the Torah.
Hallel (lit., "praise"): Read on Rosh Chodesh and Holidays.
Kaddish: Mourners Prayer.
Keter: Torah Crown.
Kiddush: Ceremonial procedure; celebratory luncheon.
Kiddush Hachodesh: Blessing the new month.
Kiddush Levanah: Blessing of the new moon.
Kippah: Head covering.

Synagogue Glossary

Kittle: Special garment worn on Yom Kippur.
Maariv: Evening Service.
Mechitza: Partition.
Mincha: Afternoon Service.
Minyan: Quorum of ten adult Jewish males.
Ner Tomid: Eternal Light.
Parasha: Portion.
Pirkay Avot: Reading from Ethics of our Fathers.
Poroches: Curtain covering the ark.
Seudat Mitzvah: Commemorative Meal.
Shacharit: Morning Service.
Shalosh Seudot: Third Shabbat meal.
Shtender: Prayer stand.
Shulchan: Reading table.
Siddur: Prayer Book.
Talit: Prayer shawl.
Tehillim: Psalms, the book of.
Tetzel: Dish for the Kiddush cup.
Tzedakah: Charity.
Yad (lit., "hand"): Hand Pointer for the Torah.
Yarmulka: Head covering.

לזכות

הרב הת׳ יוסף בן חי׳ מלכה ע״ה
מרת חנה פריווא בת אלטער יהושע הכהן ע״ה
הרב הת׳ שניאור זלמן בן חנה פריווא
חנה פריווא בת דבורה גבריאלה
הינדא גאלדא בת דבורה גבריאלה
דוד משה יהודה בן דבורה גבריאלה
מנחם מענדל בן מרים שרה
מניא שיינא בת מרים שרה
שיחיו לאורך ימים ושנים טובות

MORE POPULAR CHOICES FROM OUR "COMPANION SERIES"

The Shabbat Table Companion: Something for family and guests around the Shabbat Table!
This book will help bring the full Shabbat experience to life in your home! With clear instructions and English transliterations of all Hebrew blessings and prayers (Kiddush, Havdallah, Grace After Meals), this book is a complete guide to creating a Shabbat atmosphere in your home. *Hardcover; 6.5x5.5; 160 pages; JLG-01; ISBN 1-891293-11-7.*

The Shabbat Synagogue Companion: Explains Prayers for Shabbat Eve and Shabbat Day
A complete guide to both Friday evening and Shabbat morning prayer services, the Companion maps every prayer and explains its origin and meaning. It includes English transliterations of many key prayers and instructions for performing common synagogue honors such as opening the Ark and being called to the Torah. *Softcover; 6.5x5.5; 160 pages; JLG-02; ISBN 1-891293-12-5.*

The Complete Junior Congregation Synagogue Companion: For Children in the Synagogue
Designed for beginners of all ages, this companion brings the Shabbat synagogue experience to life. It features the basic Shabbat prayers in clear Hebrew type, alongside easy-to-read English transliterations, and easy to understand English translations and explanations so everyone will be able to join in and enjoy the prayer services like never before. *Softcover; 6.5x5.5; 160 pages; JLG-08; ISBN 1-891293-19-2.*

The High Holiday Synagogue Companion: Transliterations and Explanations
Your personal guide to and through the Rosh Hashanah and Yom Kippur prayerbook. It explains what prayers are found on each page, their origin, meaning, and the proper action required at each point, and includes key prayers as well as many inspirational readings and stories. *Softcover; JLG-03; ISBN 1-891293-10-9.*

The Passover Seder Table Companion: Transliterated Hagaddah and Explanations
The entire Hagaddah transliterated! Guides you step-by-step through the Passover Seder and all its preparations. Includes a clear and concise overview of Passover, easy-to-read English transliterations, clear instruction, plus a collection of over 50 popular holiday songs. *Softcover; 6.5x5.5; 160 pages; JLG-06; ISBN 1-891293-17-6.*

The Complete Jewish Wedding Companion: Guide to a Traditional Jewish Wedding
The ultimate guide to understanding and enjoying a traditional Jewish wedding experience. Contains clear instructions, explanations, and directions, plus all relevant prayers, liturgy, and blessings. *Softcover; 6.5x5.5; 128 pages; JLG-07; ISBN 1-891293-18-4.*